THE
KNYSNA ELEPHANTS
AND THEIR FOREST HOME

THE
KNYSNA ELEPHANTS

AND THEIR FOREST HOME

by Margo Mackay

Illustrations by Sheila Cooper Collins

Wildlife and Environment Society of SA
Knysna Centre

The Knysna Centre of the

WILDLIFE AND ENVIRONMENT SOCIETY OF SA

extends grateful thanks to

**sappi
fine
papers**

for their generous donation of paper.

This book is printed on

♻ r e v i _v_ a

made from 100% post-consumer waste.

Contributions from the following donors are deeply appreciated:

ABSA Bank
Standard Bank
Mr Stanley Wilson, CBE
Mrs M. Dormehl
Mrs U. Schultz
Telkom
Kohler Corrugated Containers
Carlton Papers of S.A. (Pty) Ltd
Falcons Equipment (Pty) Ltd
Mr B. Ochse
The photographers, who have allowed us
to use their work free of charge
All the people who bought copies of the painting,
'The Matriarch, the last Knysna elephant, the last of a great dynasty',
who as a result contributed largely to the funding of this book.

ISBN 0-620-20329-3

Published by the Knysna Centre of the Southern Cape Branch,
Wildlife and Environment Society of SA. P.O. Box 2529, Knysna, 6570

All proceeds from the sale of this book are donated to
the Knysna Centre, Wildlife and Environment Society of SA

Typesetting, printing and binding by Dando & Dando, Knysna

CONTENTS

FOREWORD

Time was when elephants meant adventure, sport, wealth. With the arrival of the first White people on the shores of South Africa, the decline of the African elephant began. For three hundred years the elephant and many other large species of game were systematically decimated. By the beginning of the 19th century, the elephant had fallen right back to the upper reaches of the Zambezi and Chobe rivers. Those that remain today in the Cape are found only in the Addo National Elephant Park and in the Knysna Forest, where there is one lone survivor of the once-great herds. That solitary animal has since been joined by two elephants from the Kruger National Park. This lone survivor is a sad symbol of man's neglect of the real world and, in our headlong rush to achieve wealth, status and position, we leave behind, either deliberately or by ignorance, much that is a part of the fabric of life and of our very selves.

The pages of this remarkable book bear testimony to those people who, over a number of decades, have fought so long and hard to preserve the last of the most southern elephants on the African continent. I am honoured to be associated with all those people who are mentioned in the pages of this book, especially Margo Mackay, who has championed their cause for as long as I can remember. I am especially honoured, for in a small way, through the Endangered Wildlife Trust and the Rhino and Elephant Foundation, I have been privileged to be a part of the efforts to ensure their survival.

There are those who will say that their passing will make no difference to the conservation of the African Elephant. They miss the point. The long-term survival of elephant in many, if not most areas in Africa, will ultimately depend upon the co-operation and goodwill of the people who live alongside them. We live in a world where man has stretched out his hand to touch the stars, where he has left his mark upon the dark, dim world of the ocean floor, and where the most inhospitable parts of the earth hold no fears for him. Happily, the pages of this book prove that man does still care; that we are not limited by self-interest alone; that we have the vision to pass this world on to the elephants and to the care of our children in a better condition than we found it.

In the end, perhaps, it does not matter why one gets caught up with elephants: they are bound to mean different things to different people. A central element of why these animals have captured our mind is, of course, their sheer size. The elephant dwarfs us, reminds us that we are fragile, even as we impinge upon its numbers and its dignity. Yet we have begun to realise the opportunity that elephants represent. Conservation of elephants means conservation of many other creatures and of their habitats, because of the very extent of the areas required to sustain such big animals. The elephant today embodies wild Africa as never before.

CLIVE H. WALKER
DOORNLEEGTE
July 1996

PREFACE

It is not easy for a small Centre of the Wildlife Society, manned entirely by volunteers, to publish even a small booklet. In 1983, the date of the first edition of *The Knysna Elephants and their Forest Home*, information was not easily available. As Chairman of the Knysna Centre of the Wildlife Society my work escalated as the Centre became increasingly involved in environmental affairs. It was only the unstinting help given by the committee at that time which enabled me to complete the writing of the booklet and enabled us to cope with the marketing of the booklet after publication while dealing with other projects on which the Centre was engaged. I should like to pay tribute to the committee members of that period: Peter and Angela Mostert, Des and Frances Freeman, Karl Hoffacker, and Margaret Addinall.

The 1996 edition of *The Knysna Elephants and their Forest Home* has also presented many problems. One complication in the writing of this edition lay in the need to add a wealth of newly acquired information to the original copy while removing material no longer relevant. Only after this had been done could the story of the elephants move on.

I am most grateful for help from the present committee members: Lorna Watt (Chairman of the Knysna Centre and the Southern Cape Branch) for checking drafts and for general support, and Gill Keown (Secretary) for advice on photographic matters and a most interesting article on the old mining days at Millwood. After thirteen years, Des Freeman is still serving on the committee

and Angela Mostert is still dealing with Centre and Branch accounts in a most expert manner. Also, Ian Withers (Vice Chairman), who, in spite of being extremely busy with the young elephants, Harry and Sally, on his farm Eden Garden where an environmental education programme is in operation, has found time to accompany me on information-gathering sorties. In addition he has spent much time liaising with the foresters at Deepwalls Forest Station on the progress of the young elephants translocated from the Kruger National Park. My thanks also to Lisette Withers for expert handling of the computer and the laborious work of packing and dispatching the prints of the Matriarch during fundraising operations.

In the 1983 edition of the book, Gillian Carter, Chief Librarian of the Knysna Library, wrote a few introductory remarks on the book and its author. In her extremely busy life she has found time to do so again for this edition. Gillian lived with her husband Nick in a caravan while he worked on the 1969/70 elephant survey. She had a front-row seat, so to speak, during that exciting time and has always been most supportive of efforts to maintain a presence of elephant in the forests. Her contribution is most appreciated.

Invaluable and much-appreciated help has been given by Eleanor-Mary Cadell, a professional publisher, who has generously advised on editing and design layout and, as a newcomer to the scene, was able to point out a few gaps in the facts and figures. Also the patient, most helpful and expert guidance given by Althia Janse van Rensburg of the printers, Dando and Dando, in typesetting and page makeup has been exceptional, and has greatly eased the difficult task of preparing the book for publication.

I thank most sincerely the members of the Department of Forestry who were unfailingly helpful, especially Dave Reynell, Forestry Information Officer, for his friendly response to my request for information, for supplying some outstanding photographs and for checking part of the text for accuracy. Also to Johan Huisamen for his co-operation.

I very much appreciate help given by Martin Lucas, Chief Forester, Deepwalls Forest Station, who interrupted his busy schedule to answer questions, read my stories on the young Kruger National Park elephants and ensure that the truth emerged from the varying accounts of their doings that were reaching me.

Grateful thanks go to the Rhino and Elephant Foundation (REF) for contributing photographs of the arrival of the young elephants. REF have been involved for many years in the problems associated with the Knysna elephants. It is therefore most appropriate and much appreciated that the Chairman, Clive Walker, has agreed to write the Foreword to this book.

Throughout the book the enchanting sketches by artist Sheila Cooper Collins bring a smile, a warmth and an appreciation of the plants and animals, large and small, that make up the fascinating world of the Knysna forests. This contribution by Sheila is truly invaluable.

Finally, my thanks to the people of Knysna, who regard the elephants with affection as part of the forest ecosystem, part of Knysna's history and culture, and who have, over the years, given such support and encouragement to our efforts to ensure their survival.

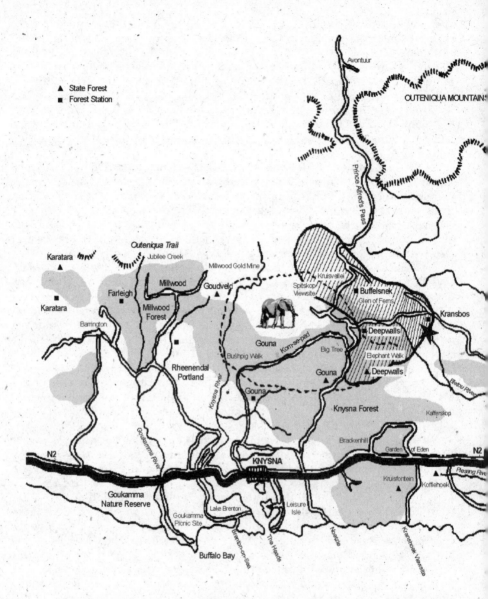

▲ State Forest
■ Forest Station

OUTENIQUA MOUNTAINS

Avontuur

Prince Alfred's Pass

Karatara ▲

Outeniqua Trail

Jubilee Creek

Millwood Gold Mine

Kruisvallei

Spitskop
Viewsite

Buffelsnek ■

Glen of Ferns

Karatara ■

Farleigh

Millwood

Goudveld

Millwood
Forest

Kransbos

Barrington

Deepwalls ■

Korrs-se-pad

Big Tree

Elephant Walk

Bushpig Walk

Gouna

Gouna ▲ Deepwalls

Rheenendal
Portland

Knysna River

Gouna

Betou River

Gouna

Knysna Forest

Kaffersklop

Brackenhill

Garden of Eden

N2

N2

Plesing River

Goukamma River

KNYSNA

Kruisfontein ▲

Koffiehoek

Goukamma
Nature Reserve

Lake Brenton

Leisure
Isle

Goukamma
Picnic Site

Brentonon-Sea

Noetzie

Kranshoek Viewsite

Buffalo Bay

The Heads

Watervalbos - a small wooded area, favourite haunt of the young elephants
and the point at which they crossed the Bitou river on to farm land.

Area visited by the young elephants in company with the Matriarch.

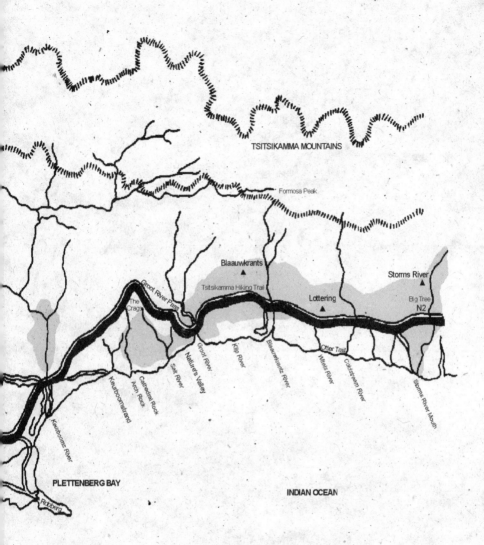

TSITSIKAMMA MOUNTAINS

Formosa Peak

Blaauwkrants

Storms River

Tsitsikamma Hiking Trail

Lettering

Big Tree
N2

Groot River Pass

The Crags

Keurboomstrand

Arch Rock

Cathedral Rock

Salt River

Nature's Valley

Groot River

Klip River

Blaauwkrantz River

Otter Trail

Witels River

Coldstream River

Storms River Mouth

Keurbooms River

PLETTENBERG BAY

Robberg

INDIAN OCEAN

Area where the 1 remaining elephant may be found.

Indigenous Forest Areas.

INTRODUCTION

When through the woods and forest glades I wander
And hear the birds sing sweetly in the trees;
When I look down from lofty mountain grandeur,
And hear the brook and feel the gentle breeze;
Then sings my soul, my Saviour God, to Thee,
How great Thou art! How great Thou art!

(Translated from the Russian by Stuart K. Hine, c. 1953)

Out at sea, the nimbus clouds form. Driven by south-easterly and south-westerly winds, they sweep in over the plateau until they hit the great mountain range which runs like a jagged spine from George in the west to Humansdorp in the east. Before rising up over the mountains, the clouds release a large quantity of moisture in the form of rain. Along the foothills of the mountains and on the plains and hills, the 'moist type' of forest, or 'high forest' as it is called, receives the rain and flourishes. Another type of forest, the 'wet forest', receives even more moisture and is found high up in the mountains or in the perennially wet ravines. This forest contains a dense undergrowth of water-loving ferns. A drier type of forest, the 'scrub forest' is found along the sea-shore or on very steep slopes. Thorns are common and the trees seldom reach a height of more than 15 metres; but the scrub forest is vital for the conservation of soil and water, the protection of plants and animals, as well as for defence against fire.

The high forest, its trees rising to heights of 15 – 30 metres, contains the famous old ironwoods, stinkwoods and yellowwoods. The Outeniqua yellowwood ('kalander') *Podocarpus falcatus* is the 'Big Tree' of the forest. It can grow to a height of more than 40 metres and reach an age of 1000 years. It is this high forest which is the home of the Knysna elephants.

The elephants are part of the history of Knysna, part of the mystique and magic of the forests where they have roamed for thousands of years, and they have always been a source of fascination and some disbelief! They are unique, not in the biological sense but because they are the southernmost elephants in the world and the only free-ranging elephants in South Africa. Even the elephants in the Kruger National Park are fenced in,

Oppsite:
Outeniqua Yellowwood
('kalander')
Podocarpus falcatus –
'the big tree of the
forest'.
(Photo: Dave Reynell)

13

although they may not be aware of it!

"Are the Knysna elephants a different species or subspecies?" This is a question often asked by visitors.

The answer is "No". In 1971 the Smithsonian Institution published a system which accepts a total of five subspecies in Africa. Our race is *Loxodonta africana africana*, the savanna elephant, whose range is taken to include South Africa, Botswana, Zimbabwe, Namibia, Mozambique, Angola, Zambia and southern Zaïre. The best known of the other subspecies is *Loxodonta africana cyclotis*, the forest elephant, from the tropical rainforests of Zaïre and throughout the forest zones of West Africa and equatorial Africa. The forest elephant is a smaller animal. It has roundish rather than 'map of Africa' ears, and thinner, shorter, straighter tusks which usually project downwards.

Podocarpus falcatus

angled → ← rounded

ELEPHANT INFORMATION

Loxodonta africana africana, showing the difference in head shape between female (angled) and male (rounded).

The period of gestation averages 22 months. The weight of a calf at birth is around 120 – 124 kg and the shoulder height is approximately 85 cm (2 ft 10 in). The calf is weaned at about the age of two years, but it may continue to suckle occasionally long after this period.

Except on those occasions when his masculinity is all too obvious, it is difficult to tell the sex of an elephant in the field since the testes are located in the body cavity. Surprisingly, the most reliable method is a study of the head. In the case of the female, the forehead has an angular appearance, whereas in the male it curves smoothly forwards and downwards. (See drawing above.)

In natural conditions, when food is abundant, a female elephant reaches puberty around the age of ten, produces a calf every three or four years and can continue breeding right up to the time of death at about fifty to sixty years of age. However, a remarkable birth-control mechanism comes into force in over-crowded conditions when food is in short supply or of poor quality. Then the onset of puberty may be delayed to any age between ten and twenty years, the frequency of calving may be reduced from one birth in every three to four years to one in eight to nine years, and breeding may cease as many as ten years before the onset of 'old age'.

Females play a dominant rôle in elephant society. A family unit consists of an adult cow and her offspring of both sexes and probably other related cows with their offspring. One cow, usually the oldest, is the leader and is responsible for the group's safety and well-being. Males stay with the female unit until puberty and then leave, or are chased out to join up with bachelor herds. Mature bulls do not stay with the family group except during breeding periods. In the opinion of the late Charles Astley Maberly, they probably dislike the noisiness of the main herd of cows, calves and young bulls!

An elephant never stops growing, although the rate of growth slows down considerably in later years. Nevertheless, the older it gets, the taller and heavier it becomes. (A bull can grow to a height of about 3,2 – 3,5 m (10 – 12 ft) at the shoulder.) Age is limited by the state of the teeth so that the legends about very old elephants of 100 years and more are not true. The elephant has six molar-like teeth which develop on either side of the upper and lower jaw. These are shed progressively during the elephant's life and at no time are there more than two of the six teeth in operation in any one half of the jaw (except in the case of young calves when there may be as many as three). As the front tooth becomes worn down or broken off, the one behind moves forward to take over. When the last molar comes into action, the elephant is probably around forty years old and when this tooth is finally worn down, the elephant is unable to chew its food and it dies.

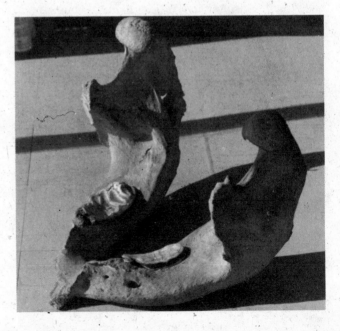

The jawbone of an old elephant, Aftand, showing the worn molars. (Photo: Margo Mackay)

INTELLIGENCE

Elephants are exceptionally intelligent. In the words of Dr Anthony Hall-Martin, formerly senior Research Officer at the Kruger National Park: "Their ability to adapt to new conditions, react to human interference and human presence, the degree of social interaction and contact which one sees among them, the subtlety of communication and the generally close knit structure of an elephant community – all require considerable intelligence to make it work. For example, an elephant does not need to 'raise its voice' as it were. It can communicate with another elephant by the slightest movement of its tail, or its ears, by a stance it may adopt, by moving its head or by the twirl of its trunk. No energy is wasted by making a point too strongly.

"Raising an elephant calf is a communal effort. Every member of the herd, particularly the females but also the young males, all help to defend and protect the youngster. In human terms, they make a baby elephant feel wanted and feel that he belongs to the herd."

A most interesting discovery concerning elephant communication was made in a United States zoo. Cornell University scientist Katharine Payne noticed a throbbing vibration which seemed to come from Asian elephants. Special recording equipment confirmed the throbbing as a low-frequency sound. A fluttering of skin on the elephants' forehead coincided with the sound. The same phenomenon – the use of a range of these sounds – was confirmed in a WWF-sponsored study in Kenya and in Namibia's Etosha Pan.

Low-frequency infrasound travels over long distances, but the frequencies are too low for the human ear. Elephants, however, can hear them and this is undoubtedly the explanation of how they can communicate over distances of several kilometres.

Young carrot fern leaf.

Opposite:
The forest at
Deepwalls, core
home range of the
elephant.

DIET

During 1979, Julius Koen, a senior research officer at the Saasveld Forestry Research Station, was commissioned to conduct a two-year survey on the Knysna elephants. Much of his time was devoted to a study of their diet and he came to the following conclusions:

- The main items in the elephants' diet are: ferns, trees – principally *Acacia melanoxylon* (alien blackwood from Australia), *Rapanea melanophloeos* (Cape beech) and *Pterocelastrus tricuspidatus* (candlewood) – and a variety of fynbos plants (the immensely species-rich, heath-like bush that forms on its own the Cape Floristic Kingdom, one of the six major floras of the world). The fynbos grasses are nutritionally inferior to the grasslands of the woodland/savanna ecosystem where grass can at times form 80% or even 90% of the elephants' diet, especially after rains when the grass is green and sweet and has a high protein content.

- In the Knysna forest area, browse (leaves) is nutritionally better than grass, but not all the plants are available to the elephants. Because of high levels of 'secondary compounds' in certain leaves, such species cannot be digested properly. These chemical compounds react with the digestive juices and render them inactive. In other words, the elephant suffers from indigestion and there is nothing like a stomach-ache to teach an animal which plants to avoid!

- Koen found that there appeared to be a phosphorus deficiency in the forest and an excess of calcium. A lack of phosphorus could be expressed in an impairment of breeding as well as a lower calf survival rate, while an excess of calcium makes matters worse by inhibiting the intake of phosphorus.

- Analysis of the plants favoured by the Knysna elephants showed them to be less nutritious than the food plants of the Addo elephants. This subject is dealt with more fully in comments on the Report by the Government.

Erica dichrus

18

Above: Lynx.

Above right: Leopard.

Right: Large-spotted genet.

Below: Honey badger.

These photographs
of forest animals
were taken at night
during a wildlife census
project employing
auto-triggering camera
units by Dr Armin
Seydack, as part of
the conservation research
programme of the
Department of Forestry.

Above: Blue duiker.

Left: Porcupine.

Below: Bushpig.

*A forest scene,
part of the elephants'
range.
(Photo: Isseline James)*

*Bushbuck ram.
Bushbuck are rarely seen,
but are plentiful in the
forest.*

RANGE AND HABITAT

The present range of the Knysna elephants, much of which is composed of dense, indigenous forest, would not under normal conditions be a permanent habitat for them. In fact, the only large animals which are true forest dwellers in this area are bushbuck, blue duiker, bushpig, leopard and vervet monkey. Bones found in the foothills of the mountains, in gardens in George and Knysna and even at the base of the Robberg peninsula at Plettenberg Bay, are evidence that the elephants once roamed over an area which included swamp, fynbos, grasslands, and forest – a choice of habitat of great benefit both mentally and physically. Then the settlers arrived. Grasslands and surrounding areas were taken over for farming, towns, roads, mining, etc. and the elephants were restricted to the forest and fynbos. Nevertheless, even in those early days, before intensive development took place, the elephants spent long periods in the forests. This was confirmed by Mr (later Professor) J.F.V. Phillips (quoted in the next section), who was stationed at the Deepwalls Forest Station in the 1920s, and travellers over the years also reported large herds in the forests. (The old name for this forest station was Deepwalls. On the first map of the Outeniqua Hiking Trail, issued by the Department of Forestry in 1979, the old name was used, but in some parts of the map, Deepwalls was changed to Diepwalle. Since that time the old name has been dropped. We feel that the loss of old names is sad, and in this book we retain the original name 'Deepwalls'.)

Journals and letters written between 1820 and 1840 frequently referred to delays between Port Elizabeth and George arising from herds of elephants blocking the road. What an experience it must have been in those early days, riding along the rough road and seeing great herds of elephant, buffalo and also eland, moving freely in a beautiful wilderness of grasslands, forests and mountains, lakes and lagoons.

E.J. Dommisse, B.A., B.Sc, former District Officer of Knysna, writing in *African Wildlife* vol. 5, no. 3, September 1951, gives some interesting information on the elephants taken from old departmental records dating back to 1877: "As early as the year 1876, Captain Harison made representations to the Cape Government that legislation be enacted with a view to protecting these elephants, as at that time he was already concerned about the rate at which they were being destroyed. In September 1877, his recommendations were turned down because it was considered hardly worth while to legislate on the subject.

"While shooting of the elephants on Crown Land was under some form of control, it was not until 1908 that the animals were declared Royal Game. Since then no further licences were issued in the Knysna area until the year 1920, when the late Major Pretorius was permitted to shoot one elephant for scientific investigation."

Although accuracy is extremely difficult in assessing elephant numbers, Mr Dommisse gives the following table taken from records:

"1870 – between 400 and 500 elephants
1902 – about 30 to 50 in the main forest
1904 – about 20 in the main forest
1908 – about 20 in the main forest
1910 – 15 large elephants and 2 young ones
1914 – 13 elephants
1920 – 7 (after Major Pretorius's hunt).

Elephants disappearing among Karri gums, (Eucalyptus diversicolor, Western Australia) in the Brackenhill Forest. (Photo: A.R. Roberts, 1962)

"The elephants are known to have roamed the forests from George to the Tzitzikama in the past, but since the turn of the century it is extremely doubtful as to whether they have visited the forests near George or the Tzitzikama. It is recorded that the last two elephants of the Tzitzikama were destroyed in the Blauberg Mountains in 1892 and the last reference to a dead elephant being found in the

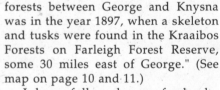

forests between George and Knysna was in the year 1897, when a skeleton and tusks were found in the Kraaibos Forests on Farleigh Forest Reserve, some 30 miles east of George." (See map on page 10 and 11.)

I have followed very fresh elephant spoor on the Outeniqua Hiking Trail just after leaving the Rondebossie hut (this is their favourite route when trekking between Gouna and Deepwalls) and also on the old Komse-Pad road. Visitors driving along this beautiful forest road are most likely to see elephant dung and even, if they are very lucky, elephants.

THE 1920s

In an article in the *South African Journal of Science* of November 1925, J.F.V. Phillips of the Forest Research Station, Deepwalls, gave the following interesting information based on records collected by him and his own personal observations while investigating the ecological and silvicultural problems of the Knysna forests. He wrote that, around 1880, the elephants roamed throughout the forest region commencing immediately west of George and extending to Witte Els Bosch in the Humansdorp Division. From references which he found in early correspondence and information supplied by reliable old woodcutters, it was clear that a secret ivory trade was flourishing. Tusks were reported to have been smuggled out of the region in wagon-loads or ship-loads of timber. The bulk appear to have been sent to the Transvaal. Half-a-crown per tusk was paid to the hunters. For such a small piece of silver were these giants of the forest destroyed.

Elephant advancing purposefully among Karri gums. Note the slight camera shake! (Photo: A.R. Roberts, 1962)

By the year 1925, it was believed that only twelve elephants remained and they confined themselves mainly to relatively small areas of forest. Other observations by Mr Phillips revealed that:
- The elephants avoid, for very considerable periods, localities where they have been molested or where their fellow-creatures have been killed or have died.
- They favour well-defined paths when moving from one area to another. These paths are usually along ridges and always cross valleys and river-beds by the easiest route. (This skill of the elephants has been invaluable to foresters who have frequently followed elephant paths when making tracks and roads. The road through the Bloukrans Pass followed an elephant track.)
- The elephant acts to some extent as an agent for seed dispersal. However, this is entirely accidental. The fruiting branch of *Virgilia oroboides*, for example, with its dry pods and small hard seeds, has no more attraction for the elephants than a non-fruiting branch.
- Regarding breeding, Mr Phillips wrote that "as

several calves have either died or been killed within the last three years, and as there are at present two comparatively young animals in the herd, breeding would seem to be progressing normally. The calves killed have been victims of the roughness and clumsiness of the adults, which have either pushed or pulled trees or branches upon their offspring by accident." ,

THEIR FOREST HOME

The animals and the forest, their days of glory and their tragic decline, go hand in hand. Exploitation of the forests started around 1763 with the coming of white settlers in the form of woodcutters, farmers and, inevitably, hunters. Before this invasion, the only human inhabitants of the area were the Khoikhoi (Hottentots) and the San (Bushmen) people. They were great hunters, but their depredations had no serious effect on the animal populations. They did, however, do a great deal of damage by starting fires in order to drive out the game. On the other hand, the white settlers had a devastating effect on all the animals. They exterminated the blue antelope *Hippotragus leucophaeus*, wiped out local populations of the larger antelope and, by 1880, eliminated the great buffalo herds even from the dense forests.

As early as 1770, timber supplies in the vicinity of the Cape were becoming exhausted. Thus, when a Swedish collector, Carl Thunberg (a pupil of the famous Linnaeus) reconnoitred the eastern and southern Cape during the year 1772 and reported on lush forests there, the rush was on. The grand old trees of the forest, yellowwoods and stinkwoods, were felled and dragged out to provide floors for houses, furniture, staircases and even railway-sleepers.

In 1811 the town of George was founded. Demand for timber increased and destruction of the forest accelerated. A year later, further exploitation occurred as supplies of timber were ordered for the Royal Navy.

Redbilled Woodhoopoe

In 1836, the Great Trek was about to begin and wood was required for the construction of wagons. The Tsitsikama (this spelling was later changed to Tsitsikamma) forests were opened up for the first time.

In 1846, all worked-out forests were closed by the Government, divided up into lots and sold by public auction. Other Crown forests were reserved and put under the control of local magistrates who were to issue felling licences. This failed to halt the destruction and in 1847 all Crown forests were closed. A Conservator of Forests, L. Haswell, was appointed to protect the reserved forests.

Captain C. Harison, Conservator of Forests from 1856 to 1874.

The protection did not last long. In 1856, there was a timber shortage and the Crown forests were re-opened. A second Conservator was appointed. Captain Christopher Harison (great-grandfather of Hjalmar Thesen, a director of the timber company Thesens Ltd) became Conservator of Forests from 1856 to 1874.

A new era might have dawned for the forests at this juncture if it had not been for the finding of gold in the Millwood area in 1860. The local population exploded from a mere handful to over 1000 people. Land was taken over for development, and pressures on all the animals and on the forests increased.

A detailed account of that dramatic and adventurous period is given by Gill Keown, Vice-Chairman and Treasurer of the Millwood Goldfield Society, which is undertaking the setting up of the mining museum at Millwood. A retired mining engineer, he belongs to an old Knysna family.

An uncle of his, who also worked on the Witwatersrand gold mines, prospected and sampled sections of the Millwood mines in the late 1930s. Based on his report, a syndicate was formed with the object of renewing mining operations in the more promising areas; but before it got off the ground he passed away and the project was abandoned.

MILLWOOD –
THE FORGOTTEN TOWN AND GOLDFIELD

'Gold is where you find it' – the message spread far and wide that abundant gold had been found in the forests and hills of Millwood, 33 kilometres to the north of Knysna. Hundreds of fortune seekers flocked there to dig for gold, many coming from as far away as Australia, California and Britain. By mid-May 1885 1400 claims were being worked on behalf of 40 syndicates. A town mushroomed almost within weeks. Six hotels sprang up, together with houses and shops, and traders flourished.

Millwood was vibrant with activity: people were born there and some died and were buried in a nearby graveyard. But within the space of five years the mushroom town had become a ghost town: too little of the precious metal had been recovered to sustain the town and its people. The disappointed diggers left and moved to Pilgrim's Rest and Johannesburg where the prospects held more promise.

When you visit Millwood now after a century of inactivity a mystical aura still seems to lurk there, as if its body has departed but its soul remains.

Because of the fascination inherent in the mysteries of history and, in this case, the enigma of Millwood, thousands of tourists and visitors descend on the site every year to relive in their imagination the activities and lives of the miners of those distant days.

Millwood Village in 1886.

In order to perpetuate the mining saga of Millwood, the Goldfields Society of Knysna is building up a museum to present visitors with a picture of the methods employed in the mining and recovery of gold. It would seem fitting therefore to include in a book on the Knysna elephants, which roamed over these gold-fields in distant times (and let it be said, many of them were shot and slain by the mining fraternity when they ventured too close to the camps), an account of its history as recorded by some of the geologists, engineers and others who were engaged in those activities.

THOMAS BAIN FINDS GOLD-BEARING REEFS

An interesting account of the finding of gold-bearing reefs at Millwood is found in a letter, dated 19 February 1876, written by Thomas Bain from Swellendam, who was the Inspector of Roads in the Western Districts. He writes that "the following is an extract from my report, dated 9 October 1871", and he goes on to say that "some six years ago I was engaged in setting out a road and cutting a bridle path through the forests and hills between the Hoogekraal River and the great Homtini River when I discovered a remarkable quartz reef of an average breadth of fifteen yards, commencing near Terblans' cottage on the farm Rooikraal, the property of the Honourable H. Barrington. It ran in an easterly direction through a deep gully, thence along the Klein Homtini and on to the Great Homtini where in the precipitous banks it ultimately disappears. It runs almost entirely under cover of dense forests, only appearing in the open near Terblans, in the form of 'white stones' so that it is unlikely to attract the eye of the casual observer. In fact [he writes] the Knysna is a most difficult country to prospect because of its rank vegetation which covers nearly all the rocks." He continues that he also found several smaller reefs in the forests.

AN OSTRICH FARMER FINDS GOLD

The first recorded discovery of gold was in 1876 when an ostrich farmer, J.J. (Cobus) Hooper, who was out gathering stones for his birds, found a nugget of gold in the valley of the Karatara River. Hooper showed his find to C.F. Osborne, a Government Official at Knysna. The find was considered significant enough by the authorities to justify an amount of £100 being granted to continue the search for gold, but in this mission he was unsuccessful. Soon afterwards Osborne was transferred to other parts of the Colony so the search for gold was postponed.

In 1880 the Cape Government Geologist, E.J. Dunn, inspected the Millwood area and so favourable was his report that John Barrington of Portland was appointed the first Mining Commissioner of the Knysna goldfields. Very little progress was reported, however, until Osborne returned to Millwood in 1885 when he began carrying out much strenuous prospecting work. He located a promising gold-bearing reef in the eastern tributary of the Karatara River.

Early in 1885, a few months after the Witwatersrand was proclaimed a goldfield, the Cape Government, after much procrastination, allowed prospecting to proceed. It seems that their diffidence resulted from the fear that there might be a repetition of the Natal fiasco of the early sixties when, according to Captain Lindley who reported on the matter, hundreds of Australian diggers were induced to make a futile voyage from Ballarat and Bendigo to the Umtwalumi and Umzinto 'goldfields' on the south coast of Natal.

In that year, 1885, over 2000 reef and alluvial claims were pegged on the Millwood goldfields, and an output of 656 ounces was announced. Numerous companies were formed, such as the Knysna Consolidated Gold Mining Company, which had an office in London, the Oudtshoorn, the Howard Farrar, the Kowie, Beaufort West and Swellendam Gold Syndicates, the Courtney-Pioneer Company, and the London Knysna Gold Prospecting Association. These enterprises, situated in the beautiful and romantic regions of forest and mountain, never developed into a second Rand, in spite of some enthusiasts declaring that the Millwood fields would outrival anything in the Transvaal!

THE START OF ORE CUSHING

No heavy crushing of ore was done until December 1887 when the Oudtshoorn Company erected a ten-stamp battery. An adit 100 feet long was driven by the Courtney into the hillside, while several other companies were reported to be doing productive work. In this year a recovery of 335 ounces of gold was recorded in the returns of the Inspector of Mines. There were as many as 600 miners, as well as some 400 other permanent residents in Millwood village, in which 135 stands were proclaimed. The tent town had given way to brick and galvanised-iron structures, with six hotels, namely the Central (reputed to be the poshest), Millwood, Commercial, Howell's, Pioneer, and Holt's Temperance, presumably unlicensed! There was a post office, a bank, and a government office, as well as numerous shops. It even sported a music-hall and three newspapers were printed.

DIFFICULT TERRAIN FOR MINING

The Millwood fields lie in the Outeniqua Mountains,

shut off in the north by high, grass-covered ridges with
many picturesque peaks rising to heights of about 4000
feet (1220 metres), and in the south by lower hills
covered by dense forest. The ground around the
goldfields lies on steep slopes and, to indicate the
difficult mining conditions the terrain presented,
Thomas Bain had this to say regarding C.F. Osborne's
proposed method of prospecting the area, which was to
sink deep shafts and install pumping machinery to keep
the shafts dry: "Nature has done the digging for us as
the following will give you some idea: The tract of
country between Hoogekraal and Homtini which I
always considered most promising is about 16 by 10
miles in extent. It is drained and rent asunder by the
following – Hoogekraal River 480 feet deep; Geelhout
Boom River 250 feet; a small gully at Olivenbosch 80
feet deep (this gully has promising indications); the
Karatara River 300 feet deep; a gully near Terblans 550
feet deep; Little Homtini 250 feet; and finally the Great

Cape Robin
in the forest leaf litter.

Homtini, 520 feet deep, which is so narrow that it looks
as if you could almost fire a charge of slugs across it
from bank to bank. The precipitous banks of these
rivers and their beds ought to be carefully examined and
a few tons of the quartz crushed and tested. The large
reef previously mentioned is doubtless the source of the
nugget found, as Terblans' house, where it first shows
itself, is on the watershed of the Karatara River, in
which the gold was first seen."

REASONS FOR THE FAILURE OF THE MINERS

While the inaccessibility of the reefs was one of the main
reasons for the unsuccessful exploitation of the goldfields, another was the woeful lack of knowledge of the
owners, managers and miners of the mode of occurrence
of the gold and its subsequent displacement by faulting,
erosion and leaching. The men appointed as managers
were experienced in professions and trades of every
description but that of goldmining, and this applied as
well to the men given the job of opening up the mines
and doing the actual mining.

Another factor which militated against the successful outcome of mining operations was the unsuitable
and prejudicial set of government regulations, as
pointed out by Osborne. He noted that the Government were probably as anxious as anyone else to have
regulations which would cause the fields to be rapidly
developed; indeed (he said) "the Government may be
considered to have a special anxiety in this regard as
they, up to the present, were the only institution which
has reaped any substantial benefit from the fields,
namely £15 000 in licence fees".

Too many of the claims were lying idle, largely

34

because they had been bought for speculative purposes and as the policy of "jumping" was not permitted, nothing could be done about the unworked claims. Originally, the Mining Act had laid down that when claims were left unworked they "shall" be declared abandoned by the Government, but at the instigation of a group of speculators, Parliament was induced to amend the regulation and substitute "may" for "shall", with the consequence that the "jumper" – a man wanting to work a claim which, although owned, had lain idle or abandoned for months and years – had first to make an application for the claim he wanted, and then wait for the Inspector of Mines to give notice to the absentee owner. The absentee owner easily overcame this inconvenience by sending someone to work for a day to "keep the claim open". Then, not only would the jumper be done out of the claim, but the owner would be reassured of its potential value because of the jumper's interest in it, and cling to it more tightly than before. So the Government continued to collect licence fees although production of gold was at a minimum, and this state of affairs certainly did not induce capital to flow into the enterprise.

Arum lily frog

There was a clamour for radical reform to induce the Government to shift the emphasis onto gold production and away from income accruing from licence fees, so that every claim not being fully and constantly worked should, by a fixed date, be declared abandoned and available to anyone who wanted to work it. The response by the Government to these inducements is not recorded.

THE TAILING OFF OF MINING OPERATIONS

Mining for gold in the Millwood area finally ceased in 1905 after 19 years of work, during which a total of 3170 ounces of gold was recovered (as recorded in the reports by the Geological Commission of the Cape of Good Hope). The successes and failures of the syndicates in their efforts to recover gold are indicated in the following summary of gold registered at Millwood during that period.

From 1887 to 1893 the average annual recovery was fairly constant, at about 330 ounces. Then in 1894 it fell to 166 and to 22 ounces in 1895. From then until 1900 the yearly output averaged 88 ounces, and from 1901 to 1905 a mere 34 ounces. No major operation could survive this low return of income so the inevitable happened and the goldfields closed down.

After 1893 very few of the mining community remained at Millwood and those who did confined themselves to cleaning up whatever gold they could find in alluvial diggings, mainly around Jubilee Creek and the Red River, west of the Homtini. From about 1000 residents who had lived in the village at its peak, the number dwindled to little more than 100, with the population in the following year dropping still further to 75, and occupying some 27 houses compared with 137 at Millwood's most populous period. The business sector diminished in proportion, with two shops and one hotel, the Continental, remaining, and the once bustling post office was reduced to a postal agency. Thus the Millwood goldfield, which had promised so much had yielded so little, with the "paths of glory leading but to the grave". In fact, the most prominent landmark remaining at Millwood is the cemetery, situated a short distance from the village, and which was allowed to become derelict and overgrown with grass and weeds. A few years ago it was tidied up and the intruding alien trees removed, so that it again depicted the hallowed ground that the bereaved mourners would have wished it to be; and the tombstones, still standing there, but draped with moss and showing mouldy evidence of long ago, bear adequate testimony to those for whom the bell tolled.

THE RESTORATION OF MILLWOOD'S MINING PAST

Although Millwood did not reach any great heights as a successful mining venture, it was nevertheless a significant event in the lives of the people of Knysna and those of the adjacent district. For one thing, it promoted Knysna as a port — so much so that at the height of Millwood's activity, some twelve vessels a month docked in the lagoon, unloading mining machinery and other mining requisites, and shipping out timber, largely in the form of yellowwood railway sleepers. Because many consider it incongruous to mine gold in the hills and forests, where the louries croak their raucous tale and, in flight, display the ineffable beauty of their green and scarlet plumage, it was felt that the forest should remain a place of tranquillity and peace. Visitors should not be reminded of rattling jack-hammers and ear-shattering blasts of dynamite, but view Millwood as historical, so that future generations would not be deprived of the memory of this vital segment of our past. What better way to accomplish this than to set up a mining museum, consisting of the reclaimed, restored and re-erected components of the desolate mines of Millwood?

To accomplish this, the Department of Forestry undertook to reclaim from the depths of ravines and river beds the rusty remains of the machinery used more than a hundred years ago, but abandoned because there was no further use for it. This reclamation was started in 1987 and it was hoped that from the wide extent of old mine workings all the components necessary to build up a complete gold recovery plant would become available. An inventory of these requirements was drawn up and the foresters, while going about their normal duties, kept their eyes open for abandoned machinery and noted its location. In a place known as the 'Golden Gully' a portable steam engine was found. Made by Ransome, Simms & Jefferies of England, it was complete and in an excellent state of preservation, even having most of its coat of paint and lining still visible; and there was enough of the century-old grease in its bearings to enable it to be towed on its own wheels for a distance of 12 kilometres to the site on the Bendigo Mine. Following up on the identification number stamped on the

Knysna Lourie

machine, we ascertained that it was supplied to an agent by the name of Schiffner & Co, Rosario, in 1894. As a 10 H.P. machine, designed to burn straw, it had a bigger fire-box than the standard coal-burning type, and as it could also steam up on wood, it was ideal for use in the forest where this fuel was obviously plentiful.

At another almost inaccessible site on the Homtini River where the Courtney Gold Mining Company once operated, more heavy mining machinery was found nestling among tall indigenous trees of Rooi Els, Cape Holly and Kershout, as well as in thick bush. At the water's edge solid concrete foundations were visible, and lying around were steel shafts, massive cast-iron bed plates and boiler shells, while partly submerged in the river was a large steel drum, and a shaft with a huge spoked pulley two metres in diameter. To add some levity to the scene, as the contents no doubt did to the miners so long before, empty brandy and wine bottles were scattered around, as well as other bottles of various shapes and sizes, but conspicuous among them were a few narrow, dark blue ones, those which once contained the mothers' palliative, castor-oil!

RECOVERING A STAMP BATTERY

Luckily, included in the party of foresters was an engineer who had the imagination to recognise in all the shafts, cams, wheels, tappets, square-headed bolts and iron rods, a complete stamp battery. The frame-work which had held the parts together had been constructed of timber, and with this having rotted away, the various components had collapsed into a pile of rusty metal. It was noted with curiosity that when a piece of this timber was whittled away it exuded a strong smell of turpentine, confirming that it was Oregon pine and not indigenous timber. The function of a stamp battery (also known as a stamp mill) is to reduce the size of ore still further, after the large rocks have been crushed in a jaw crusher (or rock breaker). It was an effective machine in the reduction of ore, with a purpose similar to that of a pestle and mortar. There were generally five or ten crushing stamps in a battery, which in California, was known as a "mortar". In more modern times these machines have been superseded by large cylindrical ball-mills which are driven by electricity.

Above:
A portable
steam engine
was found in
Golden Gully.
(Photo: Judith Hopley)

Left:
Steam engine being hauled
out of Golden Gully –
a most dangerous
operation.
(Photo: Judith Hopley)

Bottom left:
Approaching the shed
where the engine will be
housed within the
museum complex.
(Photo: Judith Hopley)

FINDING A WHEELER GRINDING AND AMALGAMATION PAN

Lying in close proximity to the stamp mill was a large steel drum, in the centre of which was a substantial shaft with a bevel gear-wheel and various other components. This turned out to be a Wheeler grinding and amalgamation pan, an essential item in the gold-recovery process. It is used by loading the pan with skimmings or blanket scrapings and adding water to make a pulp. After grinding, the pulp is heated by steam directed to the false bottom of the pan, and then a cupful each of saltpetre and sal-ammoniac is added together with 50 lbs of mercury. After being amalgamated for three hours the pulp, now very fine, is further diluted with water. At the same time a few handfuls of caustic lime are added which greatly assists the coagulation of the particles of mercury. The diluted pulp is agitated for about twenty minutes after which it is discharged from the bottom of the pan.

Above:
Stamp battery
with 5 stamps

Right:
Peripatus

Below:
The restored Wheeler
pan with steel side

A noteworthy feature of the shaft and bevel gear mentioned above is that it weighed about three and a half tons. How it was lowered into position 300 metres down an almost vertical mountainside, with the limited means available at the time, is difficult to imagine. Certainly, its recovery was a lot simpler as a helicopter was commissioned to do the work, but even so the shaft had to be cut in half to ease the load.

The reclamation of the machinery necessary to finish the plant has already been done, and most of it has been erected. Still to be rebuilt is the Robinson tandem compound steam engine, but this has been complicated because many of the smaller parts and gauges, being made of brass and copper, were very attractive as souvenirs. As usually happens in cases like this, the stable door was closed after the horse had bolted, because only afterwards was the enclosing shed finished and locked; but it has put a stop to this irksome habit. A smaller shed has been built adjacent to the larger one to house the electric generator set, which will supply electricity for the illumination of one or two adits in the Bendigo Mine. Also remaining to be constructed are the coco-pan tracks leading from the mine workings to the recovery plant, as well as a bypass track to the waste rock dump.

In the first phase of the Millwood project which started in 1987, the Forestry Department was in sole charge and carried out the work with its own staff, but later, when more mining and engineering knowledge and experience was needed, a committee was convened in 1988 and included persons with these qualifications.

Initially, the Forestry Department carried the cost of the project and did a tremendous amount with limited funds. From Messers Urbans of George they obtained various old items such as shafts, pulleys and rails, and when the Parkes timber factory in the centre of Knysna was demolished to make way for new development, additional items of antique machinery were donated by Group 5 towards the restoration of Millwood.

With the privatisation of State assets, it was necessary for the responsibility of carrying on the project to be transferred to the private sector, and funds to continue had to be found. The committee was extremely fortunate and grateful to receive a substantial grant from the Gencor Mining Group for this purpose.

When the Millwood Mining Museum at Bendigo has been completed it will provide an emotive link with the past, not only for South African visitors but for overseas tourists as well. In order to ensure its continuity of tenure, jurisdiction over the Bendigo Mine has been vested in the Knysna Municipality, with the existing Millwood Goldfields Society acting as their agents to complete the undertaking.

Elegia juncea

THE FIRST STEP TOWARDS
FOREST CONSERVATION

In 1880, Count M. de Vasselot de Regné, a French forestry officer, was appointed Superintendent of Woods and Forests. This was the first real move towards conservation. Eight years later, the Cape Forest Act was passed which gave a greater degree of protection to the forests.

In 1939, the registered woodcutter system, which had been responsible for much damage to the forests, came to an end and an annuity was provided for the woodcutters. The forests were closed to all exploitation, except for the cutting of dead and dying trees and the working of windfalls. Finally, in 1964, the indigenous forest research station at Saasveld was established and effective scientific management of the forests began.

Contrary to popular belief, very little forest on Sate land has been lost. However, large areas of forest on private land were destroyed. Many beautiful old trees in and around Knysna bear testimony to those grand old days, before the forest gave way to towns and commercial activity. Patches of remnant forest, such as those at Lake Brenton, Ashmead, and near Oakhill school where a trail links this small forest with the Pledge Nature Reserve, are reminders of a splendid past. These precious remnants with their bird and animal life should be protected at all cost.

In view of the increase in knowledge in every sphere over the next twenty years, one would have expected the forest to be safe from further depredations. Unfortunately, this was not the case. A Garden Route freeway was forced on a protesting public, and this involved the loss of 50 ha of medium to moist high forest in the Bloukrans area, when the Tsitsikamma toll road was built in

Pittosporum
viridiflorum

42

1979–80. Once again the forest rang, not with the sounds of the woodcutter's axe but with the rasping noise of the chain saw as tracks were cut through the forest and giant trees fell to make way for this unwanted freeway and its ancillary roads. For the foresters this tragedy must have been hard to bear. They have under their care 45 000 hectares of indigenous forest, in addition to artificially established pine and gum plantations. The prospect of losing any of this indigenous forest, so small in relation to our total land area, and the effect of the roads on the rest of the forest, must have been, and must still be, very worrying.

FOREST MANAGEMENT

The management programme includes conducting research into forest dynamics and the regulation of timber yields. No active planting is undertaken, as the forest regenerates itself adequately. Another important aspect is the provision of opportunities for visitors to enjoy and appreciate the forest and perhaps, by their interest, to help preserve it for all time. Nevertheless, whatever activities are undertaken – timber extraction, fern harvesting, hiking, biking – the guiding principle must be sustainability. The forest comes first! However, the question must be asked "How safe is the forest that remains?"

Narina Trogon

Every year sales of timber take place: yellowwood and stinkwood are removed from the forest in order to provide timber for the furniture industry, both in South African and overseas. Although the revenue is not inconsiderable, the cost of extracting the timber may exceed the income. Care is taken to cause as little damage as possible during these logging operations, and work is always carried out during dry weather, never when the ground is wet. Specially designed, lightweight tractors are used on the forest roads and main tracks, while horses and mules tackle the slip paths. Each area of the forest has its own team of horses – the magnificent Percherons.

There is a multi-million rand furniture and curio trade always hungry for more and more timber. In the Knysna area, where natural resources are very limited, this industry is extremely important and provides work for a large number of people. There is also an ever-growing demand for high-quality indigenous timber by buyers from all over the country. So far a balance has been maintained and the Department of Forestry follows a strict consumption and replacement policy. The local industry should have priority, but there could be a temptation to over-exploit in order to supply increasing demands for timber from further afield.

There is a never-ending battle being waged against invader trees, particularly Australian blackwood *Acacia melanoxylon* and black wattle *Acacia mearnsii*. The control of these aliens represents the most expensive conservation measure in the Southern Cape Forest Region. It appears that blackwood was introduced to these regions in about 1856. Large trees of the species were present in the gardens of Knysna by 1874 and the species had been widely planted in George (Phillips, 1928).

Blackwood does not thrive in plantations, but as part of the indigenous forest it grows into a magnificent tree. A difficult balancing act has to be performed. On the one hand the very beautiful wood of this alien tree is in great demand and is extremely valuable, providing much-needed revenue for the Department of Forestry. On the other, the problem of its growth in the indigenous forest must not go unchecked.

Extraction of timber from the forest by helicopter.
(Photo: Dave Reynell)

Logging operations
in the forest involve
the help of teams of
Percheron horses.
It is a real pleasure to
watch these powerful
animals lean into a
load, muscles rippling,
as the great logs start
to move.
(Photo:
Judith Hopley)

This is hard and
dangerous work and
the men are experts.
They care for, and
are very proud of
their horses.
Not only are they kept
in splendid condition,
but they are often
adorned with some
special decorations,
such as a bow of
ribbon on the forelock!
(Photo:
Judith Hopley)

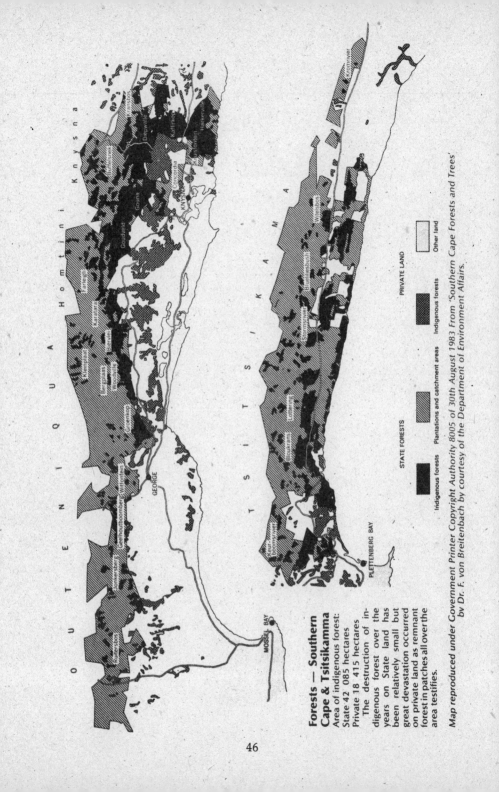

Forests — Southern Cape & Tsitsikamma

Area of indigenous forest:
State 42 085 hectares
Private 18 415 hectares

The destruction of indigenous forest over the years on State land has been relatively small but great devastation occurred on private land as remnant forest in patches all over the area testifies.

STATE FORESTS

Indigenous forests

Plantations and catchment areas

PRIVATE LAND

Indigenous forests

Other land

Map reproduced under Government Printer Copyright Authority 8005 of 30th August 1983 From 'Southern Cape Forests and Trees' by Dr. F. von Breitenbach by courtesy of the Department of Environment Affairs.

46

LILYVLEI NATURE RESERVE –
GOUNA STATE FOREST

One area of the indigenous forest that has been left in its natural state is Lilyvlei. It lies on the so-called upper plateau, between the deep valleys of the Knysna and Rooiels rivers. It is part of the Gouna State Forest, which was originally surveyed by Mr Fourcade in 1893. The Gouna Forest Reserve was demarcated by Government Notice 1049 of 1894. Lilyvlei Nature Reserve (1071.7 ha) was declared a nature reserve under the Forest Act (Act 122 of 1984) by Government Notice No 2137, on 17 October 1986.

Part of the management policy has been to reserve portions of the southern Cape and Tsitsikamma forests, encompassing all forest types and of adequate size (500 ha plus) as nature reserves. Lilyvlei Nature Reserve is one of these areas.

The primary management objective is to allow the forest to exist in its naturally dynamic state with minimum or no human interference, thereby providing a completely natural habitat for fauna and flora. It also provides an opportunity for the scientific study of unaltered ecological processes and a chance for visitors to enjoy the fascinating experience of walking in a forest virtually untouched by man. One of the most important functions of Lilyvlei is to act as a control for the monitoring of management effects in areas where resource use takes place, and also to conserve the unique Terblans beech *(Faurea macnaughtonii)* and the rare black bird-berry *(Psychotria capensis)*.

The Lilyvlei forest, because it is remote and difficult of access, has suffered almost no exploitation. In an age where ever more of our natural heritage is being destroyed, we pay tribute to the Department of Forestry for preserving such a unique area and, indeed, for the careful management of all our southern Cape forests which are a source of wonder and pleasure to all who are fortunate enough to visit them.

Podocarpus latifolius

FIRE!

In 1869 an event took place which was to have a devastating effect on the beautiful area which is now called the Garden Route and the animals that lived there – the Great Fire.

On 7 February 1869, Henry Barrington had been burning scrub on his Portland Estate. By the 9th, this fire had got out of hand. Other fires had started in the area and further to the east. There was an exceptionally hot northerly berg wind blowing. Before 8 a.m., the temperature had reached 38°C (100°F). The fires spread with terrifying speed and became a raging inferno. Bishop Gray and his wife were visiting Knysna at the time. Mrs Gray wrote: "The village had the most wonderfully narrow escape. It was surrounded, all the hills on fire, and only the narrow flat between them and the lake left – and two miles of it burnt to the water's edge – when the wind suddenly changed and carried it all away."

Twenty-seven people died in the Humansdorp area and twenty homesteads were burnt down. Many saved themselves by standing in rivers or dams until the roaring flames had passed over. So great was the devastation that many areas never recovered, people were ruined, and on the suffering of the animals it is best not to dwell.

It is not possible to track the path of the fire, which raged all along the forest belt from George in the west to Humansdorp in the east. It is worth emphasising, however, that this, the worst fire in the history of the area, failed to penetrate the main forests. The outskirts of the forests, particularly along the rivers and in the valleys, bore the brunt and were destroyed beyond recognition.

In *The Knysna News*, dated 7 May 1926, there appears an account of the loss, as a result of this fire, of two large estates: Portland, off the Rheenendal Road, and Westford in the Knysna River valley at the bottom of Phantom Pass.

The Hon. Henry Barrington, owner of Portland, summed up the work of the year 1868:

"Prosperity is dawning on Melville [original name of one of the villages at 'The Knysna']; the coast road from George to Humansdorp is, I may say, in hand. In 1870 the place must pay; the sheep are still doing well, also the cattle, the crops are good and all the family in health, thank God. Mulberry plants growing, the work for 1869 all arranged and in hand . . ."

Less than four months later, came the fire. Henry Barrington continues:

"My God, to what a state are we now reduced. Every nook of Portland is on fire. I have lost the labour and collections of a lifetime, all my furniture, all my nice library. Some small children in the Portland School house were saved with difficulty, much burned. A great quantity of forest on Portland is utterly lost, but still much remains."

In an account of a visit to Portland about this time, Bishop Gray remarks "Barrington's calmness is unruffled; he began to rebuild the day after the fire."

Some idea of the beauty of Westford, the home of Mr B.H. Darnell, is given in Bishop Gray's Journal of 1855. He writes: "On our way up to Portland, we visited Mr Darnell's beautiful farm at Westford on the bank of the Knysna River. The forest here is magnificent. We crossed the river and rode into it for some distance. The timber, chiefly yellowwood, is some of the largest I have ever seen. The trees are all very old and their forms very picturesque. Beyond the forest the mountain rises up and every here and there its crags and rocks peep out and add greatly to the effect."

In a long account of the terrible day of the fire, Mr Darnell himself writes:

". . . I had made everything so secure outside by timely burning that danger from an ordinary fire was not to be thought of. My house was situated on an elevation near the head of a small valley, widening into the large valley of the Knysna River and just opposite to its gorge, where, leaving the mountains and the krantzes behind, it ceases to be a mountain stream and pursues a more peaceful but no less romantic course to the ocean as a tidal river. No situation could be more beautiful, as those can testify who have ever looked down upon this valley from the neighbouring hills."

He described the ever-increasing density of the smoke, the rising temperature, and the increased volume of the wind. Then:

"Above the smoke I saw the liquid fire pouring over the great wooded krantzes and below it, in the fields, a great stream of fire surging along in dry grass with inconceivable rapidity. Then I knew it was all up with Westford."

Fighting against the raging wind and heat, he and the whole household, after a struggle lasting two hours, managed to reach a house which had not been devastated by the fire. Its inhabitants had taken refuge on a pontoon on the river. Later, after visiting the ruins of his beautiful farm, he writes:

"This was a clean sweep of everything – houses, trees, gardens, orchards, forest, all gone . . . Not only the natural beauties of the place, and they were great, have disappeared, but its very features seem to have changed. One might as well be on the barest Karroo place as on the banks of the Knysna. Nature neither can, nor will she, restore the grand old trees, the pride of the forest, not a few of them thirty feet in circumference, that stood on the great haugh on the side of the river opposite the house. I took a walk along the river banks; plenty of bush buck roasted alive, and I daresay an elephant or two, but not a sign of life but an old baboon crooning over the desolation, and not a sound but the crashing of trees as they fall hissing into the water."

Oh, if only we, in the 1990s, could look up the Knysna River and, instead of alien vegetation, black wattle, blackwood, rooikrans and their like, see those grand old trees stretching as far as the eye could see.

ELEPHANT HUNTING

During the 19th century, elephant hunting became a highly popular pastime indulged in by all and sundry. An expedition to the forest to slaughter elephants was the ultimate in excitement and pleasure. No thought of compassion for these magnificent animals marred the enjoyment. Typical of the attitudes of the day was a report in the *Graaff-Reinet Herald* of 9 May 1837 (available at the Millwood House Museum, Knysna). It stated that G.W.B. Wehmeyer's two younger brothers of the farm 'Dingley Dell', together with some young men from the Langkloof, went out elephant hunting and with the *35th* shot, brought down an elephant, the tusks upwards of 5 ft (1.6 m) in length, which together weighed 105 lbs (47.5 kg). The report calmly ends: "Had it not been for the rain, they would have shot more."

A ROYAL HUNT

Even the British Royal Family joined in. The *Illustrated London News* (2 November 1867) describes an elephant hunt undertaken by His Royal Highness, the Duke of Edinburgh. The party arrived off Knysna aboard H.M.S. *Racoon* and transferred to the *Petrel*, which steamed in across the bar to the beautiful inlet known as the Knysna Lake. His Royal Highness was enchanted by the scenery:

"In some places you see hill rising behind hill, like billows on the sea, each fainter in the distance, and each clothed with dark, glossy evergreen woods. In others, you have glens where lofty trees of giant growth, heavy with lichens, support their living roof of leaf-clad branches high overhead, whilst a tangled wilderness of underwood, itself composed of trees and tree-like creepers, fills the space between . . ."

Apparently it never occurred to His Royal Highness that there was anything incongruous in bringing pain and death into this beautiful, peaceful scene.

On the second day of their hunt, they found elephants in the Springfield area of what is now Kruisfontein Plantation (SAFCOL). The report continued:

The Royal Hunt. On the right, the Duke of Edinburgh, on the left, the son of George Rex.

"In an open glade, between belts of forest, eleven elephants were seen together. The proper precautions and arrangements were made for stalking them without serious risk to the hunters, and shot after shot was fired amongst them. Several were wounded, but most of the hits produced little effect. All the brutes managed to reach cover in the forest, through which they penetrated with loud trumpeting and crashing. Two of them, however, were so severely wounded, that their blood-spoor could be followed for a long distance. In fact, it is still considered most likely that their wounds proved fatal, and the hunters are now searching for the carcasses."

They tracked down two more elephants in a clump of trees: "One of the old hunters sent a mounted Hottentot boy [this was P. Stroebel, an ancestor of the Stroebel family who are famous even today for their skill as trackers] to the further corner of the clump. Suddenly and unexpectedly, he came upon one bull elephant looking sullen and ferocious as he stood there alone amid the scrub. The elephant, the moment he saw the boy, charged at full speed, gaining upon him every instant while the boy, in the utmost terror, rode towards the spot where the Prince and his party were standing, shouting at the top of his voice, 'O God, O God, Shoot! Shoot!' The Prince, however, with the utmost coolness, waited until the elephant came within twenty yards of him. One shot and then another, made the brute swerve; a volley of half a dozen bullets followed, and a final ball behind the ear from Sir Walter Currie's elephant gun brought the monster instantly to earth."

An artist's impression of the Royal Hunt in 1867.

A LOCAL HUNT

On 10 November 1884, a group came over from Oudtshoorn. After a few days of camping in different areas without finding elephant, they pitched camp in a 'nek' overlooking the Kruis River Valley. Next day elephant were found a few hours from the camp. The hunters formed into two groups. One group saw seven or eight elephants, while the second attacked a large bull, coming within 300 metres of it and the herd.

The elephants, having got the scent of the hunters, made off at a steady pace, the males on the outside, protecting the females, the large bull leading two calves. Shot after shot was fired into the bull, but he continued to lead the herd with trunk high and ears flapping. An effort was made to trace the wounded bull, but, while following his spoor, the group came across a young bull. The dogs attacked him at the head and also seized hold of his tail. With this unfair disadvantage, he was shot at a distance of 15 metres, but it still look five shots before he was brought down. The tusks of this young animal were only 18 in (46 cm) long. The young bull was skinned and that night the hunters sat down to a meal of elephant meat. Sadly, the wounded bull was never traced and we can only hope he did not die of his wounds.

A PLEA FOR CONSERVATION

Fortunately, the elephants had some friends. Captain Christopher Harison, Conservator of Forests, sickened by the slaughter, made strong pleas for the protection of these magnificent animals. In November 1876, he reckoned there were only 400–500 left out of the thousands that had once roamed the forests. Even though in 1908 the elephants were proclaimed Royal Game, the Knysna Forestry Department had virtually no authority to stop the hunters. Licences to kill elephants were issued free of charge in Cape Town without any inquiry and frequently without the knowledge of the Knysna authorities.

Over the next 30 years, the elephant population declined until in 1910 there were only 40–50 animals remaining. Captain Harison's successors repeated his pleas for conservation but the Colonial Government was not interested.

THE LAST HUNT

By 1920, the elephant herd had declined still further and only 20 animals remained. Now came another blow from which the Knysna elephants would never recover. Major P.J. Pretorius, who had wrought such havoc among the Addo elephants, received permission to shoot one Knysna elephant "for science" to determine whether or not these elephants belonged to a separate species.

During the Addo slaughter, Major Pretorius had promised the South African Museum in Cape Town "tuskers of the most abnormal proportions". In an article in *Cape Wild Life*, March 1959, entitled 'Pretorius – the Addo Elephants and the Knysna Herd', H.G. Jarvis tells the story: "But they [the tuskers] did not arrive.

Instead, a motley collection of comparatively small animals was consigned, without tusks; and when the tusks did arrive, nothing would fit the skeletal heads so far received.

"Which fitted what, nobody was ever able to discover. Gone was Pretorius' vaunted reputation as a methodical hunter and skinner.

"Considerable correspondence ensued between the various museums and Pretorius. The museums were being called on to pay high prices for the trophies by Pretorius and they considered they were not getting a square deal. Where were the big tuskers promised and what was the use of a jig-saw puzzle where nothing matched?

Lynx

55

"Pretorius had promised big elephants. They did not exist at Addo. Perhaps to assuage injured pride, and the slaughter at Addo now completed (with only 11 wild and savage survivors remaining), he applied for permission to shoot one animal in the Knysna area."

Unfortunately Pretorius had his way. "On 1st July 1920, a telegram was despatched to Pretorius on the authority of the Provincial Administrator, stating that the Conservator of Forests at Knysna was to facilitate his visit in every way and concur in 'shooting one' animal if necessary. If at all possible, make it one old bull because the number remaining is very small."

Yet there was another side to this extraordinary man's character. During the killing of the Addo elephants, he wrote to the Museum: ". . . Of course I an still trying my utmost best to save as many elephant as I possibly can by other means. I have invented a trap to catch from the smallest to the biggest elephants. This trap is now under construction in the Railway workshops at Uitenhage and should be ready in the course of ten days and will then start trapping. I hope to be able to transfer at least ten fairly large-sized elephants to the Knysna Forest . . ."

An enthusiastic letter supporting this idea was received from Dr Péringuey of the South African Museum, but unfortunately nothing further was ever heard of the scheme.

The hunt, which was to seal the fate of the Knysna elephants, started on 11 July 1920. Major Pretorius was a great showman. Several people, including some women, asked if they could go along to watch and to this Major Pretorius gladly agreed. The cavalcade, which started from the forest station at Millwood, also included two huge dogs, a photographer and all his 'cine' apparatus.

Miss Cuckoo Lister, one of the party, gave the following account, which was reported in the Knysna Millwood Museum newsletter:

"On Sunday Morning, 11th July 1920, we climbed up the little hill above our camp and there on the opposite slope across the river was the whole herd feeding in a glade between the two little forests in the kloof. The Major quietly arranged matters, told us where we could stay to watch the proceedings, out of range of bullets, and he, Mrs Pretorius and Mr Albrechts the photographer, took up their positions in the opposite glade, the

elephants having moved into the forest again. We were within shouting distance and had a perfect view. John Keet and Mr Rabbets, the Forester, then took a tribe of beaters round the top of the forest to the next glade on the left and there, in some thick bushes, suddenly came face to face with the whole herd.

"One cow elephant charged them so John fired at her and wounded her and then we saw the whole herd career down the slope and dash into the forest near Pretorius with the dogs after them and all the beaters and us yelling for all we were worth. Soon after, the great bull emerged, just below Pretorius, and he fired at it in the back so as to get a good cinema picture. It dashed on across to the next little forest in spite of another bullet in the head. Meantime, to our horror, another huge chap came out about 30 yards above Major and Mrs Pretorius, so we yelled and they looked round to find the elephant charging them. The cine was quickly concentrated on that and Pretorius fired. The elephant turned and also made for the forest, the Major, his wife and the cine man hard on his heels. They put an

In the year 1920, Major P.J. Pretorius was given permission to shoot one elephant "in the interests of science".
Five elephants died as a result of this hunt. (Photo: Archives of the Department of Forestry)

end to him and then hurried down and finished off the other one."

A further account of this hunt appeared in the *Cape Argus* of 24 August 1929, written by Francis Newdigate:

"Trees began to sway and shake, dogs started yelping madly, people shouted and then, as the noise seemed to be at its height, the heavens were rent with the most terrible racket imaginable – the fierce trumpeting of elephants in distress, for the dogs were attacking a cow and her calf, and the mother was furious. The herd made for fresh cover.

"Silence reigned and we all looked tensely at Pretorius. He was still in the same position, apparently not the least affected by the scene which had taken place. As we gazed, out into the open walked the most magnificent elephant we had ever seen and at the exact spot which Pretorius had anticipated, not 50 yards from him. This, then, must have been the bull that Pretorius had hoped to get. The sight of the Monstrous animal and the wiry little man facing each other was a contrast never to be forgotten. Neither feared the other and as the bull walked past, ears extended and trunk held high, there was contempt for man in every stride he took.

"Then the cinema got busy and Pretorius stepped out. BANG! and a cloud of dust appeared on the elephant's back where the bullet struck it. With a sort of stumble the old bull continued his walk. BANG! and yet another BANG! but the large bore, high velocity express elephant rifle seemed to have little effect. At last, just as he was about to enter the forest again, the 8th shot brought him down. Pretorius jumped on his body and stood there in triumph. The bull raised his head to look at his gloating enemy, rolled over on his side and died without a sound or a struggle, as became the passing of so noble a creature.

"Upon Pretorius returning to his post, another bull appeared which he likewise dispatched in about 6 shots."

During this inglorious hunt a cow was also shot and confusing stories surround the incident. In her classic story of Knysna and Plettenberg Bay, *Timber and Tides*, Winifred Tapson gives what is undoubtedly an accurate account of the tragedy:

"The story of the shooting of the cow was given me by one of the chief actors in the drama. A calf had got into difficulties down a steep krans and to save it from falling to its death, he and one of the beaters went down to help it up. While engrossed in this errand of mercy they suddenly found themselves overshadowed by the great bulk of an angry mama intent on demolishing them. They fired and headed her off. During that night she was seen to pass by in the close vicinity of the hunters' camp, and was found dead of her wounds the following day, twelve miles distant from the scene of the tragedy."

Her calf and another were also later found dead. Thus five elephants died as a direct result of this hunt. These are harrowing stories, but they are part of a shameful history and they pay tribute to the bravery of the elephants and their care of their families, even under fire.

ELEPHANT SURVEYS

In January 1968 the Eastern Cape branch of the Wildlife Society of Southern Africa (the Knysna Centre was not founded until 1976), concerned by the lack of information on the elephants living in the Knysna forests, commissioned three of its members, J.L. Smuts, J.H.M. David (zoologists), and G.B. Keeping, to carry out a short survey to determine, if possible, whether a long-term investigation would be justified.

Hoopoe, seen on the forest fringes.

The results of this survey, which lasted only ten days, were remarkable. During this action-packed period it was established that at least two adult bulls, a male teenager, two cows and a calf still remained in the forest. To this number could be added the legendary bull, 'Aftand', who was known to exist: although he was not encountered on this occasion, he was seen quite clearly by Graham Keeping and his family during a later visit to the forest.

There were many exciting moments during the short survey, but quite the most dramatic was the story of tracker John (Aapie) Stroebel and the enraged elephant cow. This is told in Graham Keeping's report:

"This elephant happened to be a small cow and what she lacked in stature, she made up for in fury.

Above:
John 'Aapie' Stroebel,
a well-known tracker
and descendant of the
P. Stroebel who acted
as tracker for the
Royal hunt in 1867,
was engaged to
accompany the team.
Aapie is now living
in retirement at
Harkerville.
(Photo: Ian Withers)

Opposite:
". . . she reached up,
the sensitive tip
of her trunk
curling this way and
that as she tried
to grasp Aapie's
thrashing boot."

"Aapie had found recent spoor and hoped that it would lead us to the old loner 'Aftand', whose name was always on the foresters' lips. He went off to reconnoitre and returned to announce that he had found a cow and calf. This was news. We bundled off into the forest, hurriedly snatching up the usual paraphernalia. Aapie relieved me of my old army haversack containing the hired still camera as I was already encumbered with the cine and accessories.

"We did not have far to go and in very little time were moving cautiously forward, acutely aware of an unfavourable breeze. Aapie stopped near a scattered group of Witels trees. Through the thick tangle on the sloping ground before us we discerned the rounded rump of an adult animal. Then to the right a miniature trunk curled upwards above the bush – her very small offspring. The breeze now blew across us so Smuts and I moved round to get more downwind, leaving Aapie and David at the tree. On resighting we saw the larger trunk of the cow rise purposefully and point ominously towards our group.

"The next moment the silence of the forest was shattered and bedlam broke loose. There came the sudden flurry and crackling of splintered trees, and we heard the sound of her rapid advance as she bustled full-tilt up the slope, bashing everything down in her path.

"Cramming my Bolex cine into the pocket of my shorts, I scrambled up a narrow sloping branch of the neighbouring Witels tree. I selected badly and straddled insecurely some ten feet above ground. The head and shoulders of the cow emerged from the bush. She had short white tusks. Now after all the rush, she stopped, uncertain of our exact positions, some ten paces from the tree behind which Aapie and David remained hidden.

"David took her portrait as she stood there clearly weighing up the next move. Struggling to maintain balance, I feverishly attempted to extract the cine camera, which was wedged, turret upwards, in my straining pocket.

"From this point onwards all further thought of photography was forgotten. Aapie had started to climb,

and as the cow moved forward again, accelerated his ascent. The haversack and camera dropped to the ground. He had just cleared some 12 feet when she charged. Pounding the ground she reached up, the sensitive tip of her trunk curling this way and that as she tried to grasp Aapie's thrashing boot. The forest became pandemonium. Shrill trumpeting mingled with Aapie's vain howls of 'Skiet hom, skiet hom'. Unfortunately for him there was nothing to 'skiet' with. We were unarmed. Attacking from another angle, the cow then charged the tree, backed and charged again, Aapie clinging on for dear life. The tree creaked ominously. The elephant's tusk ripped off a large portion. She charged for a third time. As she thundered towards him Aapie knew this was the moment of truth. Neither he nor his tree could withstand such an onslaught. Then suddenly on reaching the tree, she sheared off and disappeared into the forest. Why? Perhaps she remem-

Baby elephant (6 weeks old) killed by a falling tree in the Harkerville Forest in 1968, thought to be the offspring of the enraged cow. (Photo: Dr F. Rousseau)

bered the calf in a nearby glade and maternal instincts prevailed.

".The three of us gathered below the tree. Aapie still hung on, dazed and unable to believe that the crisis had passed.

"Below the tree, stamped down into the soft ground was the haversack. We pulled out a battered camera."

Shortly after the Smuts/Keeping/David survey, Major Bruce Kinloch, formerly Chief Game Warden of Uganda and Tanganyika, was asked by the Department of Nature Conservation of the Cape Province to carry out a ten-day survey to establish the number, and if possible the sex, of the elephants still surviving in the Knysna forests. In addition, he was requested to determine whether there was any truth in the theory that they are a distinct subspecies – all this in ten days!

Thus, in February 1968, armed with a considerable store of information from foresters and others intimately acquainted with the elephants and accompanied by trackers Aapie Stroebel and his nephew Willem, Bruce Kinloch embarked on his formidable task. Only his extensive experience of elephants and other big game and the skill of the inimitable Aapie Stroebel could make this assignment even partly attainable.

In an article in the magazine *African Wildlife*, vol. 22, Bruce Kinloch had this to say:

"I could state categorically that, at the time of my visit, there were at least seven elephants of varying age groups in the Knysna forest, indicating slow but regular breeding over the years. On all the evidence, my estimate of total numbers was at least ten. The old bull, of which I had been lucky enough to get some unique photographs, though a massive elephant, was no bigger that other fine specimens of *Loxodonta africana africana* that I have seen elsewhere in Africa."

It was a remarkable achievement and the conclusions drawn were in accord with the previous survey and borne out by Nick Carter's survey in 1969/70.

It was decided that the results of the two surveys amply justified carrying out a lengthy, in-depth investigation.

B. (Nick) Carter, a professional game warden with considerable experience of working with elephants in the Kruger Park and with big game in Kenya, was appointed to undertake the survey in co-operation with the Department of Nature Conservation and the

Department of Forestry. The now famous tracker, Aapie Stroebel, and his son, Anthony, were added to the survey team. The terms of reference were:

1. To ascertain numbers and composition of the herd
2. To observe feeding habits and migrations
3. If possible, to find the reason for low breeding rate or lack of fertility
4. To establish whether the animals are a subspecies or variant of the bush elephant, *Loxodonta africana africana*
5. To make recommendations for future conservation.

The survey would last from February 1969 to January 1970.

One of the Knysna elephants photographed in 1968 by Graham Kepping.

Aftand – too close for comfort.
(Photo: Major B. Kinloch, 1968.)

DANGEROUS?

Nick Carter had been warned that the elephants were vicious and dangerous. This was simply a case of 'give a dog a bad name' and in his report, Carter wrote: "I conclude the survey by stating quite seriously that I have never come across such a civilised group of elephants in all my career, with the possible exception of those who used to wander happily around the Park lodges at Murchison Falls in Uganda. Here, in spite of the undoubted persecution which they have experienced in the past, they have worked out for themselves a relationship with humanity and its side effects to their own satisfaction. I have watched them under just about all possible conditions and even in some of the deepest and furthest kloofs, the noises of traffic and industry can be heard in the background. Among the plantations the disturbance can rise in decibels to amazing heights before they get fed up and wander off. I say 'wander off' because there are rarely any signs of panic unless caused by a sudden and unexpected fright."

In his final report on the survey Carter gave the following information on the elephants he had studied during the year-long survey:

"Their eyesight is certainly much keener than any other elephant I have encountered and has on several occasions proved most disconcerting. With the wind blowing strongly in my favour on the sea cliffs, I have been spotted instantly by a cow, once at sixty yards and on another occasion at about two hundred yards. It may be possible that their long sojourn in the forest gloom has sharpened their eyesight to this interesting degree."

The following details show the composition of the herd:

ELEPHANT DOSSIERS

Number	One [Aftand]
Sex	Male
Age	Over 45
Height	10' 6'' [3.2 m]
Tusks	Left 60 lbs, Right 70 lbs approx. [Left 27 kg, Right 32 kg]
Spoor	Front foot 19 x 16'', Rear foot 20 x 12'' [Front 48.3 x 40.6 cm, Rear 51 x 30.5 cm]
Dung	Large bolus, badly digested
Ears	Not ragged. Bullet hole high up in left ear.
Knysna Characteristics	An inveterate digger of fern roots. A pronounced upswept curve on left-hand tusk. Good eyesight.

Knysna elephants photographed by E.M. Williams during 1970.

Cape grey mongoose

Critical Line	About 35 yards.
Remarks	An even-tempered animal with remarkable traffic sense, as witnessed on the national road. Completely blasé of human sounds and activity. Probably gave rise to the original legend of 'Aftand', because of his broken left tusk.
Number	Two [Blackberry]
Sex	Female
Age	Around 10 years
Tusks	Light white ivory of about 15 lbs [6.8 kg] each.
Spoor	12 x 9″ and 14 x 9″ [30.5 x 23 cm and 35.56 x 22.86 cm] Both feet very similar.
Dung	Small, well digested.
Knysna Characteristics	A digger. Good eyesight. Left-hand tusk slightly upswept.
Remarks	Usually accompanied by a young bull and a cow who may be her mother.
Number	Three [Elderberry]
Sex	Female
Age	20 approx.

Paradise Flycatcher

Tusks	A little over 20 lbs [9 kg] a side.
Spoor	16 x 10″ and 16 x 12″ [40.64 x 25.4 cm and 40.6 x 30.5 cm]
Dung	Well digested, small bolus.
Knysna Characteristics	A digger. Upswept left-hand tusk. Very good eyesight.
Remarks	Critical line of 70 yards [64 m] or more. Seen frequently with a large young bull. Possibly pregnant. Aggressive and dangerous.

Number	Four
Sex	Female
Age	Not known. Fully adult.
Spoor	17 x 14″ [43.2 x 35.6 cm] front foot.
Dung	Adult, well digested.
Remarks	Only glimpsed once or twice. Believed to be the mother or 'auntie' of Blackberry (No. 2)

Number	Five [Champion]
Sex	Male
Age	25 years or more
Tusks	Between 50 and 60 lbs [22.7 kg and 27.2 kg] each side. Yellow ivory. Sharply pointed.
Spoor	17 x 14″ and 18 x 12″ [43.2 x 35.6 cm and 45.7 x 30.48 cm].
Dung	Large bolus, well digested.
Height	11′ 3″ [3.4 m].
Knysna Characteristics	An upswept curve on the left-hand tusk.
Remarks	The largest animal of the whole group. Frequently seen in the company of Elderberry (No. 3).

Number	Six [Booytjie]
Sex	Male
Age	Forty or more years
Tusks	40 lbs [18.14 kg] each side approx.
Spoor	18 x 14″ and 20 x 12″ [45.7 x 35.6 cm and 50.8 x 30.5 cm].
Dung	Adult, sometimes badly digested.
Height	Ten feet [3.05 m].

| Knysna Characteristics | Upswept curve on left-hand tusk. |
| Remarks | A quiet but suspicious animal. Tail almost hairless. Tattered and hairy ears. Right-hand tusk has had point broken off at some time. |

Number	Seven [Hairy Ears]
Sex	Male
Age	Around fifty years
Tusks	Right-hand 40 lbs, left 50 lbs [Right 18.2 kg and Left 22.7 kg]. Right-hand tusk broken.
Spoor	17 x 14″ and 19 x 12″. [43.2 x 30.5 cm].
Dung	Medium bolus, sometimes poorly digested.
Height	10′ 6″ [3.2 m].
Knysna Characteristics	Upswept curve on left-hand tusk. Good eyesight.
Remarks	Hairless tail and hairy ears. Tattered ears. Quiet animal.

Number	Eight [Youngberry]
Sex	Unknown
Age	Under five years
Spoor	7 x 6″ [17.8 x 15.2 cm].

Profile of Hairy Ears. The broken tusk extends only as far as the trunk. The complete left tusk can be seen sticking out behind the trunk. (Photo: Archives of the Wildlife Society)

Dung	Small, well.digested.
Height	Perhaps a little over 4 feet. [1.2 m]
Remarks	Rarely seen. Spotted once by the Survey Team and on other occasions by reliable independent witnesses, in the indigenous forest above Brackenhill. Spoor measured at Harkerville on the Klein Eiland track. Its mother still keeps it in the depths of the forest as a rule.

Number	Nine
Sex	Female
Age	Adult, fully grown.
Dung	Well digested
Remarks	The mother of Youngberry (No. 8). Once seen momentarily by the Survey Team. Keeps to the loneliest forest with her calf. Dangerous and has been known to charge.

Number	Ten
Sex	Male
Age	Young adult
Tusks	About 30 lbs [13.6 kg] a side.
Knysna Characteristics	Left-hand tusk upcurved.
Remarks	Usually moves around with Blackberry (No.2). Only seen clearly twice in Harkerville.

Number	Eleven
Sex	Unknown
Age	Born March 1970
Remarks	Not seen as yet.

"There is no discernible evidence of low fertility in the group. Their numbers have not increased as they appear to have been killed by illegal shooting. Protection is not afforded by declaring them protected unless an official is appointed to ensure this."

Carter and his trackers studied the elephants almost every day for a year. In spite of the difficult conditions of thick forest and limited visibility, they had managed to locate and observe different groups which, in the

light of the enormous difficulty experienced ten years later in even finding the elephants, was a remarkable achievement. Carter was convinced that poaching had taken place, but felt that indiscriminate shooting by smallholders posed as great if not a greater danger. In fact, just such an incident took place in his presence during the survey. (Further confirmation was provided during a visit I paid to an old woodcutter in the Deepwalls area of the forest. He told me about the elephants breaking down his plum trees and admitted to shooting at them (that incident occurred around 1976). He said ferociously, "If the elephants come here I shall shoot them.")

Carter pointed out the dramatic increase in numbers of the Addo herd as soon as they were fenced, and urged that a special fenced reserve be provided for the elephants in the Harkerville Forest. He concluded:

"The slenderness of the thread by which this little group of elephants hangs on to its existence must be emphasised. The urgency for conservation measures must be stressed. A special reserve in this holiday and tourist area would be an important asset in the future."

The report was discussed at a special meeting of

Aftand.
Note the sunken area on the head, denoting an old elephant.
The left tusk was not much shorter than the right. (Photo: B.V. Bredenkamp, 1970)

Doublecollared Sunbird

professional biologists on 30 October 1970 when some
of the recommendations were modified. The final
discussions took place at the Knysna Elephant Conference held in the Port Elizabeth Museum on 25
November 1970 and attended by senior representatives of the Department of Forestry, Cape Provincial
Council, National Parks Board, local government
bodies, scientists, the Wildlife Society, and other
interested persons. The general opinion of the
conference was that the elephants were living in
equilibrium with their environment, that the breeding
rate was normal, that poaching had not taken place,
and that there was no need for a fenced reserve.

At the end of the conference in a final summary of
three years' investigations, the Wildlife Society had
this to say:

"It was most gratifying to hear from the Department of Forestry that they had instituted far-reaching
plans for the conservation of the entire ecosystem of
the Knysna area under their control, and that the

indigenous forests, approximately 67 000 acres in extent, had been classified as a Nature Reserve. Emphasis had moved from plantation silviculture to multi-purpose use, which includes paying increasing attention to the indigenous flora, research work on both flora and fauna, including elephants, and amenities for the public.

"In view of this important information, the Society is satisfied that the elephants will have ample space for their habitat, and the need for enclosure of a limited area has fallen away. In a further categorical announcement, the Department of Forestry stated that they accepted responsibility for the elephants on State-owned land, and would act as guardians for their conservation . . .

"The Wildlife Society is most gratified with the results of three years' intensive work carried out on the Knysna elephants. This work initiated by the Society has clarified most of the problems which had been posed regarding the elephants and their conservation. The wide public interest aroused by the Society on the future of these animals, and the care now promised by the Forestry Department will assure their well-being for posterity."

In view of the subsequent history of the small herd, this confidence turned out to be sadly misplaced. The recommendations in Carter's survey reports were ignored.

Over the years, the Committee of the Eastern Province Branch of the Wildlife Society had done its best to save the elephants. It had spent time, money and effort, culminating in this very effective and comprehensive survey. What a pity there was no follow-up.The following questions could have been asked of the Department of Forestry:

• Had someone been detailed to keep a full-time check on the elephants and monitor their movements? Would regular reports be issued on the condition and numbers of the herd?

• Had steps been taken by the authorities concerned to prevent shooting by smallholders?

Erica

73

• Were there any open areas available to the elephants? (Past history showed that areas of fynbos
greatly favoured by the elephants had been taken over
one by one for plantations, until the elephants were
virtually walled in by alien trees. If they ventured
outside this prison in search of a change of diet, they
were shot at.)

Tolerance by the elephants of human activities as described by Nick Carter applied only to normal sounds and behaviour in the forest. Any question of serious tracking was quite another matter, as Hjalmar Thesen found out. He had received a report of an elephant in the forest nearby and had gone in with a forest worker who appeared to know where the elephant was. They quickly picked up the spoor and soon noises of branches breaking warned that the elephant was just ahead. Hjalmar told the story during a radio interview:

"All I saw of him was a trunk stuck up like a periscope, obviously smelling or looking for me, so I crouched down in a little patch of bracken and stayed there for some time. He was very close by and I could see his eye and a piece of tusk. Then he suddenly moved off and vanished. There was a rustling of leaves. Summoning up my courage, I crept closer. Meanwhile my little companion had disappeared so it was rather lonely out there. I followed along the track and eventually emerged onto a logging road and there was the old elephant walking along in front of me. I tiptoed along behind and took a snap. At this he became aware of my presence and turned off into a patch of thick bush. I could just see his great bulk standing sideways on with enormous tusks sticking out. They seemed to me very long indeed and I was determined to get another picture. I stepped out from behind the tree where I had been hiding. He immediately, with a most dramatic movement, stepped right out into the open and looked straight at me. His ears went out, his trunk went up, he gave a tremendous squeal of rage and came straight for me. It was a moment of absolute horror as this great tank-like creature came thundering down on me. Of course the instinct is to turn and run and this I did. As I ran the ground fairly shook as the great animal thundered along behind. I kept running until I was so exhausted that I fell into a stream and was immensely relieved to find that all was peaceful and quiet again." (This incident took place in the 1960s.)

It has been said that foresters are not the best people to look after elephants since their great love is trees and it is their business to protect them, whereas all too often it is the business of elephants to destroy them. Yet there are many foresters who care deeply for the animals of the forest and have a particular affection for the elephants. One such forester was Alton Roelofse, who came to Knysna as Manager of Thesens' Brackenhill Forest in 1952.

Over the years, Alton Roelofse had many adventures with elephants, but the most extraordinary encounter occurred when he and his wife went off for a fishing trip.

It was one of those misty early mornings. The windscreen of the old fishing buggy soon became smeared with moisture, which reduced visibility to a minimum. They turned off the main road towards Brackenhill Falls and then drove down the firebreak which runs alongside the power lines towards Plettenberg Bay, en route to their favourite fishing spot.

The banks on either side became very steep and visibility worsened. Alton decided to try the screenwipers although in such conditions, the wipers often made matters worse. He leaned forward, but before he had time to press the switch, there was a bump and they came to a sudden stop. The car had collided with the back legs of an elephant, the bumper gently hitting him behind the knees! The occupants of the car froze and waited for furious retribution, but to their stunned amazement, the elephant just kept on walking. As soon as he had disappeared in the gloom, Alton got out and scrubbed away at the windscreen with a handkerchief. Then, to his horror, the elephant reappeared, looming up out of the mist and heading straight for the car. There was no time to escape. The elephant came right up to within a trunk's length of the bonnet, then, completely ignoring the rigid human figure, turned and scrambled up the bank. That particular part of the bank was the only place within quite a distance which was fairly easy to climb!

In his amusing and informative book *The Elephants of Knysna*, Nick Carter tells the story of the survey. The following remarkable incident occurred during a time of persistent raiding by the elephants. He writes:

"On the forest edge at Koffiehoek lived a forest worker called Kassie. He was a short, stocky little man with a cheerful grin and a surprisingly good command of English. He was also a good gardener and the odd acre around his forestry-owned house was kept in excellent order by a tribe of women, children and other hangers-on, who attacked the ground furiously when necessary and produced between them some very fair crops of vegetables.

"One familiar member of this household was the dog, which was the usual mixture of breed and patchwork colour and intensely disliked the survey team; although I doubt if there was anything personal in the dislike. It just hated all strangers and made its loathing quite clear.

"Kassie's chief problem just now was the bushbuck, who crept out of the forest edge in the dark and raided the young vegetable plants, causing minor but persistent damage. Not possessing even an 'anti-elephant shotgun', he did the next best thing by posting the hound at the top end of the garden with a box for a kennel. To ensure that it did not abandon its post, he fastened it with a running wire to another longer wire, which covered the whole of that part of the vegetable patch and which was suspended from the two poles. All went well for a week until the elephants moved over into the Koffiehoek area, about the time of our arrival on the scene at Harkerville.

A peaceful scene of river and forest in the Goudveld area. (Photo: M. Mackay)

Milkwood.

"One night the raiders crossed the start line on the forest edge and selected Kassie's garden as their objective. As the first elephant came through the scanty hedge, Faithful Fido gave tongue furiously, but incautiously in view of the fact that he was tethered. One of the intruders turned on him instantly – elephants hate dogs – and pursued him up and down the length of the retaining wire.

"I could reconstruct the affair in my mind's eye, from Kassie's description and from the confused footprints, fresh in the mud: the elephant striding to and fro, tossing its trunk and flapping its ears as it made repeated jabs with its tusks at the dodging animal: the dog, panic-stricken, its barks turning to yelps of fear as the wire halted its flight each time: faces peering fearfully from the shack window, a hundred yards away, wondering what was happening up there in the dark.

"At last the wire broke, probably snapped by the elephant's legs, and the hound was free. Here came the moment of truth for Kassie and his family. The dog bolted down the garden path, making straight for the flimsy tin and matchboard shack, its known home and refuge, while behind it thundered the elephant in hot pursuit. For some reason known only to itself, it did not try to hide from its five-ton assailant in the hut, but, perhaps impelled by overwhelming fear, dashed on past the dwelling and on to the Koffiehoek road.

"The enraged elephant following, and now certainly dropping behind for elephants cannot run very fast or far, lost the yelping nuisance on the road and turned away with disgust into the forest, tearing down a blackwood tree in passing, as though to vent its anger on something that it could get hold of. Peace of a kind descended. The other two elephants followed on through the garden and ate some of the maize.

"The dog was found near Kafferskop the next day..."

Ian Withers, manager of the farm Eden Garden, on behalf of the family trust, is the author of the following amusing elephant stories told to him by his grandfather, Daniel Muller. Born Henry George Godfrey Daniel Miller, the German-style 'Müller' was entered in error on his birth certificate. It was easier and cheaper to drop the dots over the 'u' than change the name back to Miller, so Muller it remained.

"As a young boy growing up on the edge of the Eastern Cape bushveld in the village of Redhouse a short distance from Port Elizabeth, I grew to love the bush and all its secrets. Some school holidays were spent at Brackenhill outside Knysna with my grandparents. My grandfather was employed by Thesens and in the 1930s lived at the Crags where he managed the trading store as well as the plantation, including the large Zoetkraal farm. (Barlows recently donated this area purchased from Thesens to Nature Conservation.) When he moved closer to Knysna to manage the Brackenhill store and forests for Thesens, he also moved to the area known to be a favourite haunt of the elusive elephants. His love for these giants of the forest was apparent, and as a young boy on vacation from Redhouse, I always wanted to listen to the latest news on the elephants.

"Oom Dan, as my grandfather was affectionately known, was kept up to date about the elephant movements in the forest around Brackenhill by the local people, foresters and a young man called Alton Roelofse, who had joined Thesens to manage their Brackenhill forests in the early 1950s."

THE ELEPHANT AND THE BICYCLE

"One afternoon after work, so the story goes, a young labourer was cycling home through the forest with his faithful fox terrier running alongside. Suddenly the dog darted into the forest and started barking at some unseen object with tremendous fervour. The young man thought nothing of his dog's antics and continued pedalling on homeward. The dog's yapping grew fainter the further down the road he cycled, but then suddenly he heard the alarmed screams of his canine friend accompanied by the trumpeting of an enraged elephant. He looked around and caught sight of an enormous elephant exploding from the dense foliage onto the road. Stricken with fear, the young man began furiously to pedal as fast as his legs would allow. This extra exertion on the bicycle caused the chain to jump from the sprocket. Without resistance, his legs pumped like pistons – there was now no longer any means of forward propulsion. Meanwhile, the little dog was gleefully gaining on his master where surely he would be safe. Unfortunately, so too was the enraged elephant rapidly bearing down on both bicycle and passenger. What fear must have gripped the unfortunate young man as he helplessly free-wheeled down that forest track, losing speed rapidly while shouting at his confused dog to get away from him. As the bicycle slowed, the chain dangling uselessly from the sprocket, terror gripped him. It was now a matter of pure survival. Jumping from the bicycle, he sprinted into the safety of the dense undergrowth.

"The wheels were still spinning as the elephant came thundering up. Luckily for the fugitive, the elephant vented his anger on the bicycle, tossing and trampling it beyond recognition."

THE ELEPHANT AND THE PUPAE

"My grandfather's uncle, Percy Tait, who had an insatiable passion for hunting and fishing found a ready companion in his young nephew. And so it was that my grandfather and great great uncle made ready one evening to hunt bushpig on a near-by farm known as Sandriffies, owned then by Dr Viljoen and adjoining the Garden of Eden. Sandriffies had a magnificent Dutch-gabled dwelling at the end of a long oak-lined roadway and Dr Viljoen grew the loveliest of juicy apples, which he proudly exhibited very successfully overseas at annual shows. The elephants thought these apples were also the best they had sampled and it was here under the oak trees that a most unusual meeting between man and beast would occur.

"To hunt wild pig successfully one should be in position during the hours of darkness – say from 9 p.m. onwards – and remain as quiet as possible. The pigs loved the acorns that fell from the huge old oak trees during autumn and the early months of winter. This hunt was not the first, nor would it be the last, these two adventurers embarked on together. For this reason two grain bags had been secured to the boughs of one of the old oak trees as hiding places some time during the previous acorn season. These sacks had served them well, as was borne out by the lovely wild-pig roasts that had been enjoyed by both families. It was here that these hunters made their way, clambering up the rough plank ladder to settle themselves in their tree cocoons

Striped mouse

some four metres above the ground. Twelve-bore shotguns were loaded with A.A.A. shot cartridges and held ready for the unsuspecting wild pig as both men silently sat in ambush.

About an hour had passed when the hunters became aware of approaching noises among the dried oak leaves – the moment of truth had arrived, and they thought the long wait was nearly over as they cocked their weapons in anticipation. However, they also detected low rumbling noises which they'd never associated with their prey before – could it be elephants? It was! Blinding fear gripped them as they realised that they could be detected by the three elephants now looming into view below them. Suddenly the tree began to shake and vibrate as one of the elephants rubbed his thick hide against the old oak. Acorns rained down on the heads of the human pupae in their cocoons – they would have to climb higher into the protection of the tree if they wanted to be safe from the reach of the elephant's trunk. Almost as one, both hunters stood up in their grain bags, the hunt suddenly forgotten. Being the younger and fitter man, my grandfather reached safety first. His uncle, though, was not so fortunate. In his haste to escape, the grain bag was strained to breaking point and, with a loud ripping and tearing sound, spilled its contents onto the unsuspecting elephant's broad back below.

"The shotgun, still firmly grasped and cocked in Percy Tait's hand, now went off, the pellets causing more acorns and leaves to rain down upon this sorry lot. All hell broke loose as the elephants stampeded, trumpeting and screaming into the night in one direction, while Uncle Percy took flight to who knew where in the other. When he eventually stumbled to a halt, he was completely without breath and had no idea where he was. It was not until after sunrise the following morning that, bruised and lacerated, he was able to find his way home."

Patricia Storrar, in her book *Portrait of Plettenberg Bay*, tells what must be one of the first stories of the Cape South Coast elephants ever to emerge from the early days. The story concerns the flamboyant French traveller, François Le Vaillant.

She writes: "In the vicinity of Plettenberg's Bay 'into which the waters of the Queur Boom and the Witte Drift fall', Le Vaillant added to his collection several fine birds, including a male and female of 'the beautiful kind of Balbuzard, which is a species of the eagle' (the Fish Eagle). His Hottentot trackers and servants caught several buffaloes, large herds of which came to graze on the other side of the Keurbooms River within sight of the camp.

"On 25 June, having enjoyed a month in this lovely area so rich in game, fish and birds, the Frenchman decided to continue his journey, but found it impossible for his wagon to get through the passes (eastward or northward? We do not know) and so returned to Die Poort. As he was walking along in this direction he saw an elephant's spoor which he judged was not more than a day old. With four of his best Hottentot marksmen he set out to follow the elephant's tracks, persevering until nightfall when 'we made a large fire, supped gaily and laid ourselves down to sleep upon the earth'. They awoke at daybreak and Le Vaillant having given his hunters a glass of brandy each in the dawn light, they followed him 'with pleasing alacrity'.

"There follows the first and most dramatic account of the shooting of an elephant in these parts. François Le Vaillant was, of course, the hero of the chase. 'I soon got near enough to one of these enormous beasts, and instantly firing my carbine lodged the contents in his head; he staggered and fell; the rest, about thirty in number, ran from the place as fast as possible.' After describing in detail his escape 'by falling down by a trunk of a great tree' from another huge beast which had been wounded by the Hottentots, he continues, 'The report of my piece was a universal signal of joy; and I was presently surrounded by my people. The affectionate Klaas knew not how to express his satisfaction; he pressed me eagerly in his arms . . . Klaas was now my brother.'

"As night was drawing on they returned to the camp. The Hottentots quickly kindled several fires, cut slices off the elephant to broil for themselves and dressed a part of the trunk for Le Vaillant. He was delighted. 'It was the first time I had tasted this kind of food, but I determined it should not be the last, as I thought it delicious.' But better was still to come. Klaas assured the Frenchman that the elephant's feet were even more tasty than the trunk and to prove it, prepared them for breakfast the next morning.

"The method they used was this: 'They dug a hole in the earth, of three or four feet square, which was filled with burning wood, covered over with dried branches, so as to keep a very brisk fire a good part of the night. When they thought this pit sufficiently heated, the fire was taken out and the four feet being placed in it, were covered over with warm ashes, then with lighted embers and some small dry sticks, which continued burning till morning.' François, the sybarite, was the only one who slept that night, as Klaas and his other men kept watch over the fire till morning. They heard elephant and buffaloes during the night, but the fires apparently kept all wild life at a distance.

"At breakfast time Le Vaillant was presented with one of the elephant's feet. 'Dressing had prodigiously swelled it, but it exhaled such a savory odour, that I soon tasted and found it to be delicious . . . I could not conceive that so gross and heavy an animal as the elephant would afford such delicate food.' The explorer's enthusiasm for this new dish knew no bounds. 'Never', said I, 'can our modern epicures have such a dainty at their tables; let forced fruits and the contributions of various countries contribute to their luxury, yet cannot they procure so excellent a dish as I have now before me.'

"So ended what was undoubtedly the first elephant's foot braaivleis to be enjoyed by a White visitor in the Plettenberg Bay area."

DEATH OF AN ELEPHANT (1971)

During Nick Carter's survey, several distinct elephant personalities emerged, the most impressive being the old elephant he named Adam. Adam was prepared to come out into the open from time to time and he became, certainly in recent years, a much-photographed elephant. Hovering like a ghost in the background, though never seen by the survey team, was the legendary figure known as Aftand (broken tooth), a sort of 'Moby Dick' of the forests. The trackers firmly discounted the possibility that any of the elephants they had seen could be Aftand, but Nick eventually decided that Adam and Aftand were one and the same.

Aftand was a mischievous animal, with little fear of humans. From time to time he raided smallholdings and destroyed crops and trees. Sometimes he amused himself by pushing over the log seats and tables provided for visitors' picnics. The solution could have been to fence off the smallholdings, an action which would have benefited the entire herd. Unfortunately, it was not considered worthwhile to spend money on fencing and, in 1971, a senior official in the Department of Forestry (Dr F. von Breitenbach) ordered that the old elephant be shot. No doubt aware of the public outcry which would erupt if this deed became known, an

Aftand emerges from the forest. Note the bullet hole in his left ear. (Photo: B.V. Bredenkamp)

attempt was made to conceal the death of Aftand. It failed.

A first-hand account by Nick Carter of the court case that followed appeared in *African Wildlife*, vol. 28, no. 4:

"The utter shambles that preceded, accompanied and followed this incredibly inefficient operation was presented remorselessly in the George magistrate's court when the Doctor and his two assistants managed, somehow, to get themselves into the dock on a charge, among other things, of hunting protected wild animals!

"I state categorically that the George courthouse has never seen a trial like it and never will in any foreseeable future.

"I myself was called as a witness. Other members of this great crowd included Dr von Breitenbach's second-in-command, the overall Director at Knysna, a member of the Thesen family, and an almost Shakespearian cast of foresters, attendants, and, dare one say it in the Shakespearian sense, clowns? There was also the farmer who had lent the gun that fired the eventually fatal shot. It was a nine point five Mannlicher-S, which is known to the professional hunting and game warden fraternity as 'The Worst Of Them All', because of its low velocity and ponderous bullet.

"The hunt had been conducted throughout with this piece of ordnance and an old .303 which refused to go off when the trigger was pressed on at least one occasion.

"As an ex-professional game warden, it was easy for me to criticise this inept hunt, but my real complaint against the Doctor is that 'Aftand' was the only one of the Knysna elephants at that time which could have been drug-darted. Here a golden opportunity was missed. The animal could have been put to sleep, thoroughly examined by experts from all circles, and his vital statistics compared with other members of *Loxodonta africana*. He could have then been given the antidote and it would have been quite likely that, on awakening, the fright of the knowledge that something untoward had occurred would have sent him far away up into the Gouna forests. If it had not and he had returned to his habit of raiding forest-edge gardens, then he could have been darted again, this time with a fatal dose and left to die in his sleep.

"The whole trial took about nine days and the

magistrate in his summing up said astringently that it could have been completed in two. On a straightforward technicality the accused were eventually acquitted, but in the course of rending one another gave an exhibition of Forestry Department laundry that had the spectators gaping. They have since left the Knysna area, and the Department, pulling up its socks, renewed its promises concerning the safety of the elephants and took the praiseworthy step of appointing one of its officials to concern himself especially with the fauna of the forests, the nearest we have come to getting a much-needed, full-time game warden."

Sadly, this promise was not kept. No forester was appointed to pay special attention to the elephants. Had this been done, the tragedy of the decline of the small herd might have been avoided. Nick Carter's recommendations were generally ignored.

A GRIM ANNOUNCEMENT (1980)

Little was heard of the elephants after this incident until 1980 when the Department of Forestry announced that only two elephants, a cow and a calf, could be located in

" . . . he could have stepped from his tree onto her back!"

the Knysna forests. In 1979 Julius Koen had been asked to do a survey on the elephants. After months of work, which included two occasions on which over 200 forestry workers combed the forests in search of the elephants, the total tally still remained two. A few days after the last search, Koen, with one forester and two trackers, found the cow and the calf, but this time they were in the company of an old bull.

During this search there were moments of considerable excitement and danger. On one occasion, Julius Koen, Coert Geldenhuys, also of Saasveld, and the two trackers, were observing the cow and calf in thick bush. Julius climbed a small tree in order to get a better view. The rest of the party remained on the ground. Suddenly Coert signalled to Julius that the cow had picked up their scent. Without warning, she charged. The ground party fled, but Julius had no time to descend from his tree. The cow stopped right beside him. So close was she, he could have stepped from his tree onto her back. Luckily, she was obsessed with the scent of the ground party and was not aware of Julius. He held his breath, not even daring to blink until the cow moved off – a very close shave.

A REWARD IS OFFERED (1981)

In May 1981, deeply concerned at the plight of the elephants, the Knysna Centre of the Wildlife Society held a committee meeting at which Nick Carter, who had conducted the elephant survey in 1970, and a member of the Department of Forestry, were present. At that meeting it was decided unanimously to offer a reward of R50 for any evidence leading to the discovery of elephants, other than the three already known to exist, or of bones of dead elephants. This offer was published in the local Press and the national newspapers also picked up the story. The reward was deliberately not large since we did not want a crowd of holidaymakers tramping around the forest and possibly

"No sign of the Knysna elephants, but we've found some tremendous yellowwoods!"
(By the late John Jackson of The Argus – *Cape Town.'*

*Young bull,
age about 12 years,
emerging on to the forest
road near the big tree
in the Deepwalls area.
(Photo: Kito Erasmus,
1982)*

*Kito Erasmus and
his party ventured too
close. The young bull
gave chase and skidded
to a halt when he had
"seen them off".
Kito and Shona Winde
examine the elephant's
dung and skid marks.*

endangering themselves. It was directed primarily at forestry workers, who might do a little exploring in their free time, or who might be in possession of untapped information. Unfortunately, there was no response and it is possible that the workers, many of them living in remote areas, and not avid readers of the newspapers, were unaware of the offer.

THE ELEPHANT WORKING GROUP

A total of three elephants! Yet ten years before there had been at least ten.

As a result of a recommendation by the S.A. Nature Foundation, the Minister of Water Affairs, Forestry and Environmental Conservation established a Working Group whose task it was to investigate the whole situation, decide what had caused the decline in the number of elephants, and recommend a course of action. The following people were appointed:

Dr A.J. Hall-Martin – National Parks Board
Dr G.L. Smuts – Natal Parks Board
Dr D.J. Brand – Director: National Zoo, Pretoria
Mr J.H. Koen – Directorate of Forestry
Mr J.D. van Wyk – Department of Nature and Environmental Conservation, Cape Provincial Administration
Mr C. Walker – Endangered Wildlife Trust
Prof. R.C. Bigalke – Forestry Faculty, University of Stellenbosch
Mr K.H. Cooper – Wildlife Society
Prof. J. du P. Bothma – University of Pretoria
Mr P.J. le Roux – Directorate of Forestry, Head Office, Pretoria, Convener and Chairman

The Group met twice, at Knysna, on 25 February 1981 and from 13 – 15 April 1981.

In considering reasons for the decline in numbers, two main factors emerged:

Harassment – shooting at the elephants to drive them off private property, and poaching.

Restricted habitat – the effect on the health of the elephants through being confined to the forest and having access to a much more limited variety of food than in earlier days.

91

HARASSMENT

Up to as recently as 1977, members of the herd trekked in spring to the sweeter veld of the Harkerville Coastal Forest and back again to the Deepwalls/Gouna Forest for the winter. Suddenly this trek ceased and the elephants were seen no more in the Harkerville Forest. It is reasonable to suppose that harassment was the prime cause of this change of pattern, particularly sniping at the elephants by plot owners, which was known to have occurred. Increasing traffic levels may also have acted as a deterrent.

It might be thought that if an elephant were shot, the carcass would be bound to be discovered. This is not necessarily so. An elephant, seriously wounded, would probably seek solitude and water down in one of the deep kloofs. If this happened, his death would not necessarily be discovered since these remote kloofs are rarely patrolled and some are completely inaccessible.

While compiling this book, the author spoke to many people intimately associated with the forest in search of a solution to the sudden disappearance of the elephants. Their opinions fell into three categories:
a. Sniping by smallholders, the wounds eventually proving fatal.
b. Poaching by forestry officials who had the knowledge and the opportunity to get away with it.
c. The elephants, or some of them, are still there, hidden away in the remoter areas. (This seems unlikely in view of the recent intense searching.)

RESTRICTED HABITAT

It is accepted that a habitat which is restricted to the high forest and fynbos may not be ideal, but to what extent, if at all, it militates against the successful breeding and general good health of the elephants, is debatable.

Nick Carter reported that there was no discernible infertility in the group and that the breeding rate appeared normal, as far as such a term could be used for so small a group of elephants. He went on to say that they were the fittest and fattest elephants he had ever seen. Mineral licks put down on elephant paths during his survey were not used, nor were the many oranges strewn about in their favourite haunts.

Elephant crossing the old N2 from Harkerville to the Garden of Eden. The elephants would wait for long periods hidden in the bushes until satisfied that no vehicles were near before crossing the road. They would have had a problem with the racetrack which is the N2 today. (Painting by Eric Wale)

Dr Anthony Hall-Martin, who has studied elephants over many years and is South Africa's leading authority, said in the Fauna and Flora Preservation Society's magazine *Oryx* of August 1980: "The Knysna elephants when seen are invariably in good condition, as were the animals in 19 photographs that I have examined . . ."

John Phillips, Professor of Botany at the University of Natal and formerly of the Forest Research Station, Deepwalls, (quoted earlier) said in his introduction to the final Conference on the Elephant Survey in 1970: "We know something also about the existence of elephants in considerable numbers in the forests and related vegetation of the Transkei, Natal and Zululand. This is of ecological interest because it bears upon the setting of the elephants in what we call today the ecosystem; although these animals were frequently found in the forest climax and higher successional stages of the forest, they were also at home in the more open areas. In the George/Knysna/Tsitsikamma regions these latter areas are represented by the fynbos, whereas further to the east and on to Zululand, grassland, open woodland and thicket constitute these more open stages. We should appreciate, therefore, that the elephant along the coastal lowlands and immediate hinterland from the Cape to Natal is intimately associated with a forest and related ecosystem. Further afield, of course, the animal was, and still is, part of the wooded savanna/grassland ecosystem. I make this point because I believe it is unwise to argue that the alleged rate of reproduction has fallen low in the Knysna deep forest due to insufficient availability and variety of food."

Professor Phillips estimated during his earlier research work that by 1925 only twelve elephants remained and that *they confined themselves to relatively small areas of forest.* In other words, for the last *fifty* years the elephants have been confined to the forest *without* access to swamps and grassland, yet their numbers remained relatively stable until the 1970s.

In 1970 there were at least ten elephants, but by 1980 there were only three. Whatever the rights or wrongs of the diet deficiency issue, it is not only difficult, but impossible, to believe that during a period of ten years, seven elephants had died of malnutrition.

Finally, a comment from the editor of *African Wildlife* (Vol. 36, No. 6): "The Society does not accept that poor nutrition is the sole reason for the decline of the elephants. It is far more likely to be lead-poisoning from bullets . . ."

FUTURE MANAGEMENT

The Elephant Working Group considered various options for future management and after much deliberation, the following statements and recommendations were agreed unanimously:

1. The Knysna elephants are not a distinct subspecies and are therefore not scientifically unique.
2. The Knysna forest is of prime importance for conservation since it is the largest and best indigenous forest in southern Africa.
3. The elephants should be conserved as part of the whole Knysna forest and fynbos system.
4. In order to increase the viability of the elephant herd

People said,
Why didn't you climb
a tree? – NOT EASY!
(Photo: Kito Erasmus)

the following steps should be taken:

a. Suitable licks (probably salt) should be put out for the surviving animals since certain essential elements are lacking in the forest vegetation. Potatoes, lucerne and oranges should also be tried as supplementary food.

b. The sex of the young animal (calf) *must* be determined.

c. If the calf is a male (as suspected), then three female calves should be introduced from Addo, camped for a limited period in the main forest and then released to enable them to join up with the existing three.

d. Certain private properties should be acquired by the Department of Forestry or the State which are presently a threat to the viability of the total system.

This should also help to eliminate certain pressure points on the elephants themselves.

e. A regular monitoring programme of the elephants must be maintained so that their movements and activities can be constantly studied.

f. Certain vulnerable farming areas, i.e. to the east of Harkerville, should be securely fenced off to prevent the movement of elephants onto these lands.

5. For many reasons it would not be advisable to fence in a 5000 ha area of the forest and confine the elephants to this small area. (The main reason for this decision was the fear that extensive damage to the forest would be caused by fencing and the use of the habitat by a large population of elephants. Another possibility, that is to buy land adjacent to the forest and fence it, would be prohibitively expensive in terms of the price of land and the difficulty of fencing.)

6. For the long-term future of the elephants and other large mammals, it would be most desirable to consolidate the existing Forestry Department lands in the Knysna region to form one single large conservation area.

REACTIONS FROM THE GOVERNMENT (1982)

The recommendation to introduce three young Addo elephants was turned down by the Department of Environmental Affairs in a press release issued on 9 February 1982. The last paragraph of the statement reads: "All facets of the matter, *inter alia* the fact that the elephants have decreased in numbers over the years under conditions which will essentially remain the same despite the fact that they have been protected, have been carefully investigated by the Department of Environment Affairs and, taking into consideration all relevant facts and after careful consideration, the recommendations of the Working Group cannot be approved as far as the importing of three young elephants from the Addo Elephant National Park is concerned."

In commenting on this statement, the following points should be made:

1. The statement says the elephants were protected when, in fact, they were not.

2. The conditions under which the introduced

elephants would live would *not* remain the same if the recommendations of the Elephant Working Group were carried out, particularly items 4 (d), (e) and (f).

On receipt of this depressing news, the Knysna Centre organised a petition to test the feelings of local people and visitors on the question of saving the elephants. Over 4000 signatures were obtained which showed how strong was the local feeling that the Knysna elephants should survive.

THE PETITION

The petition was presented to our Member of Parliament the Rt. Hon. the Prime Minister, Mr P.W. Botha, by the author and committee member Des Freeman, who had led the campaign. This encounter took place in George and we were to be allowed ten minutes. Mr Botha immediately launched into reminiscences of his own encounter with the elephants:

"The incident with the elephants in the Knysna forest took place many years ago (around 1953/4) when Kruisrivier and Wittedrift were still part of the George constituency. I was returning from a meeting which I held at Kruisriviernek when a number of elephants – I think there were three or four – were lying in the road. I immediately realised that I wouldn't be able to chase them away and get past them. The result was that I had to turn back and return to Wittedrift from where I proceeded to Knysna by way of another road."

The minutes ticked by . . . Des Freeman interrupted to request that we consider the matter in hand. We had hoped Mr Botha would accept the petition himself and possibly put in a word on our behalf. The hope was in vain. We were instructed to forward it to the Minister of Environmental Affairs. In reply, the Director General of that department sent a copy of an 8-page report emphasising the difficulties which could be encountered and reasons why other elephants should not be introduced.

Chasmanthe
aethiopica

THE REPORT (1982)

The report gives a resumé of the whole position, much of which already appears in this book. It emphasises the damage which would be done to the forest if a section were fenced off as an elephant reserve. However, only partial fencing was recommended by the Elephant Working Group, and it is the reasons for the rejection of their recommendations by the Department of Environment Affairs that are of primary importance.

Let us look at the main points of the report, starting with the statement on possible reasons for the decline of the elephants from ten or eleven in 1970 to three in 1979 when Julius Koen started his survey:

- Mortality of animals due to old age and a disparity in the ratio of males to females in favour of males.
- Incorrect counting of the number of elephants.

These two issues can be dealt with together.

The 1970 survey carried out by Nick Carter involved intensive observation for a whole year. During this time he developed a most effective information service, fuelled by oranges! Oranges had been supplied to the survey team for placing on the ground in open areas in the hope of luring the elephants to places where they could more easily be observed. Unfortunately, the elephants showed no interest in the oranges, probably because they had not seen them before. (The Addo elephants became great orange eaters.) However, the children of the local forest workers soon learned that if they supplied accurate information on the movements of elephants, they would be rewarded with oranges. Thus the survey team, after checking on two or three elephants in, say, the Harkerville Forest, could move quickly to follow clues to the whereabouts of other groups in the main forest.

In his report on the survey, Nick Carter gave details which included, where possible, age, sex, spoor and dung in the case of each elephant seen. He concluded that there were three old males, including Aftand, two young males, one about twenty-five years old, another whose bolus was small and well-digested, and two more also dropping well-digested dung, indicating youngish animals. There was also a youngster aged about five years, sex not known, and a calf born in March 1970 which was not seen. That is a total of eleven elephants, none of whom, except for the three old males, was over thirty years of age. Nick Carter, as an ex-game warden, had considerable previous experience with elephants and his assessment of numbers rested not only on visual observations but on spoor measurements and dung analysis, a reasonably accurate method of determining age.

In view of the above, it seems fair to assume that there could not have been a mis-count, nor could all the missing elephants have died of old age.

The report goes into detail regarding the problems that might arise and lists various reasons why additional elephants should not be introduced into the forest.

It is inconceivable, however, that the Elephant Working Group, with its wide range of knowledge and experience, did not consider all the difficulties and objections which are included in this report. What, then, was the stumbling block which prevented the acceptance of their recommendations? We believe that the answer lies in a fear that the State could be held responsible for damage to private property which might be caused by any introduced elephants. This belief was confirmed during further negotiations between the Rhino and Elephant Foundation and the Government in 1994, when proposals to translocate young elephants from the Kruger National Park were again discussed.

Where wild animals occur in a natural habitat, e.g. the present elephants in the forest at Knysna, there is no legal obligation to prevent damage. The court could award compensation in instances where these animals cause damage, but the chances of this occurring are minimal.

Where the Department creates a potentially dangerous situation or aggravates an existing situation by a positive action, e.g. by translocating elephant from their natural habitat to a new area, there is no doubt that the Department will be held responsible for damage caused by the elephant(s). The Department will also be held responsible for compensation if they realised that the elephants could have caused damage and did not take the necessary precautions to prevent such damage.

The report concluded: "Apart from the responsibility placed on the Department as custodian of the 43 000 ha of unique indigenous forests in the Knysna and Tsitsikamma forestry areas, these areas will be protected and managed by the Department for the benefit and enjoyment of future generations."

The elephants have always been part of the forest ecosystem. Very early records report elephants in the forests. If the elephants disappear, that will mean a *change* in the system and it could well be a change for the worse. The Department of Forestry says it will manage the forests for the benefit and enjoyment of future generations. Will those future generations be happier with a forest without elephants?

Certain important recommendations of the Elephant Working Group have not been mentioned in the report. These are: the acquisition of certain private properties; regular monitoring of the elephants; fencing off vulnerable farming areas; and consolidation of existing Forestry Department lands in the Knysna region to form one single large conservation area.

Of course, consolidation costs money, but it is of paramount importance. Only 0,3% of land in the whole of South Africa is under indigenous forest. Many of the plants in this wonderful southern Cape land of forest and fynbos are unique. Scientists are constantly discovering properties possessed by plants which are of great benefit to man, but because of the continuous destruction of habitats, many of these plants disappear before they can even be examined and tested.

In recent years there has been a worldwide increase in the tourist trade, especially in eco-tourism. Visitors are looking for wilderness experiences, a chance to relax in game and nature reserves and to go on walks and trails.

There have been discussions on the possibility of combining the great beauties of the Garden Route – the forests, lagoons, rivers, lakes and mountains – into a contractual national park under the protection of the National Parks Board, Cape Nature Conservation and the Department of Forestry. Such a grand concept would provide an outstanding attraction for visitors and would create growing opportunities for the promotion of the RDP in the form of jobs as tour guides, in the manufacture of goods for sale to this fast-growing industry, and in the provision of unusual and imaginative types of accommodation – the possibilities are endless.

The contractual national park would be able to encompass within its boundaries agriculture, silviculture, development areas, towns and villages under a common policy and mutually supportive management. Co-operation with such a scheme by the different components would ensure that decisions taken remain environmentally friendly.

HOPE REKINDLED

In 1986 an event took place which would have a far-reaching impact on both the elephants and the forest. Author Dalene Matthee published a book, *Kringe in 'n Bos*. She wrote in Afrikaans and subsequently translated it into English under the title *Circles in a Forest*. It became a best-seller, not only in South Africa but worldwide. It was also prescribed as a set book for schools that year.

The book gives a fascinating glimpse into the lives of the people of that time, the woodcutters, the merchants, the gold diggers and, of course, the elephants. Woven into this tapestry runs a delicate love story – the unthinkable yearning of a poor young woodcutter for the daughter of a rich, unscrupulous merchant, one of the buyers of timber produced by the woodcutters. The book stimulated an immediate interest throughout the country. Tours of the forest were arranged, and many people including schoolchildren came to walk in the forest and follow in the footsteps of their hero and, of course always hoping for a glimpse of the elusive elephants. Most important of all, the visits to the forest, as well as the wealth of information which was provided, created some understanding and appreciation of the forest and of the elephants. It was a great help to the Rhino and Elephant Foundation and the Knysna Centre of the Wildlife Society in their unflagging efforts to persuade the Government to allow the translocation and introduction into the forest of young elephants from the Addo Elephant Park or the Kruger National Park.

Inevitably, it was decided to make a film of *Circles in a Forest*. I have never understood why some film-makers spend large sums of money buying a story from an author and then ignore the very essence of that story, the magic which made it a best-seller. There were moments at the beginning of the film when the young boy establishes a mystical rapport with the elephants and hopes for an outstanding film rose, but it was not to be. The story developed into a boy meets girl romp,

'Abu' star of the film, Circles in a Forest, feeding on the forest vegetation. (Photo: M. Mackay)

with elephants rushing around like circus animals. A great opportunity was missed. This unusual story with its fascinating historical background could have produced a world-class film, as happened with the story of Karen Bliksen in *Out of Africa*.

Nevertheless, no failure of the film could detract from those wonderful actors – Randall Moore's elephants.

Randall Moore, a geologist who had spent 20 years working with elephants, was asked to go to America and buy four elephants suitable for film work. The mission was successful and Abu, a fine 18-year-old tusker destined to play the part of Big Foot in the film, together with Sammy, Benny and Cathy were selected.

Abu and Benny had originally come from the Kruger National Park, while Sammy and Cathy had been captured in Uganda.

Randall, together with his two assistant trainers, Doug Graves from Oregon and Jo Dudley from Rockville, Maryland, and his charges, embarked from the east coast of North America bound for Cape Town. The weather was bitterly cold. Throughout the month-long voyage the elephants were secured by chains on deck. As the ship neared Cape Town stormy conditions added to their misery, the elephants slipping and slithering as the ship rolled in the big seas.

During the journey by truck to the Knysna forests it was observed that Abu was trying to support Sammy with his tusks – an action in keeping with the compassion elephants show one another. Sammy died before reaching Knysna, his death thought to be due to pneumonia caused by cold and stress. In a macabre ending to this tragedy, Sammy's body was used in the film to portray a dead elephant.

The remaining elephants settled into the forest as to the manner born. At night they were confined in a large cage, but during the day, when not filming, they emerged attached to long chains which enabled them to browse on the forest vegetation. Randall Moore reported that towards the end of their stay in the forest they were subsisting almost entirely on the forest vegetation and taking very little of the supplementary food brought in for them.

Urgent pleas were made to Government to allow the elephants to remain. Randall Moore had proposed that he should ride Abu into the forest accompanied by Benny and Cathy in search of the Knysna elephants. He was prepared to spend up to a year on the experiment, observing the behaviour of the elephants and finding out if the Knysna elephants would accept the newcomers. The introduction of mature animals would have meant that breeding could have started immediately. Sadly, it was not to be. The request was refused, and another opportunity was missed. Randall and his elephants are now in Botswana running a very successful and exclusive safari operation in the Okavango delta. Visitors ride on the backs of the elephants along trails in this magnificent wildlife wilderness. In this way they can get much closer to other animals than is possible either on foot or by car.

ELEPHANT SIGHTINGS

During 1987 several sightings of two elephants were reported and I was personally involved in one of them. I was part of a group of hikers on the Outeniqua trail and we had heard that elephants had been seen on the trail. We had left the Rondebossie hut, walked for about 30

minutes and had reached a plantation area. Lying on the path was a fresh fern – ferns rank as a delicacy on the elephants' menu. Our leader prepared his camera, not believing for a moment that elephants could really be present. Nevertheless, all talking ceased as we moved quietly round the next bend. There, on the bank above us, head protruding through the foliage, stood a large cow elephant. The shock was mutual! We stood rooted to the spot. The elephant took off at high speed, scattering pine trees as if they were matches. In the silence that followed the sound of splintering wood, we strained our ears to try to detect any further sounds of elephants but we could hear nothing. Slowly we walked a few metres further on to examine 'Susie', an old steam engine, a well-known landmark on the trail. "Look", whispered one of the party. There, further along the trail, in deap shadow, stood two elephants. After casting an unhurried look at us, they walked casually down into the indigenous forest to the right of the path. At first we thought we had seen three elephants, but a look at the photographs clearly revealed that the two elephants on the path ahead included the elephant we had first encountered on the bank. She had circled round, in spite of her fright, to stand beside her teenage companion. Unfortunately, the second photo was not clear enough to print.

No more was heard of the elephants until January 1989 when it was announced by the Department of

Forestry that a calf had been born. Its tiny footprints had been observed by foresters and the baby elephant had been seen and described by forest guards. There was great rejoicing in Knysna. But who was the father? It was thought that the old bull was past the age of breeding. In addition, he had not been seen for many months and it was probable that he was no longer alive. This could only mean that the young bull, now about 19 or 20 years old, must be the father of the calf.

THE STRUGGLE CONTINUES (1994)

The Knysna Centre of the Wildlife Society had campaigned for fourteen years in an effort to secure the future of the Knysna elephants. With so few animals now remaining, the only way this could be achieved was by the introduction of elephants from elsewhere. Further negotiations with the Government were necessary in order to move the project forward. This would mean frequent meetings to explore all possibilities and, above all, to find a way to indemnify the Government against any damage the elephants might do. (As explained earlier, the legal position changes once elephants are brought in from another area.) Since Knysna was so far from Pretoria, the seat of government, such intensive activity would be difficult.

However, the Endangered Wildlife Trust, based in Johannesburg, had for many years also been involved in efforts to save the Knysna elephants. In 1981 they, in conjunction with the Argus newspaper group, mounted a campaign which led to the formation of the Elephant Working Group. In 1988 Chairman Clive Walker, together with Dr Anthony Hall-Martin, formed the Rhino and Elephant Foundation (REF). Under the co-ordination of Vice-Chairman John Ilsley, REF intensified its efforts to resolve the difficulties.

ELEPHANTS FROM KRUGER NATIONAL PARK

SUCCESS FOR REF

It took nearly a year, working with the Wildlife Broking Services, to achieve sufficient public indemnity to satisfy the Government. At last their efforts were rewarded and agreement with an insurance company was reached. On 26 April 1994, the Minister of Environmental Affairs announced that approval had been given for the introduction of two young elephants from the Kruger National Park into the Knysna forests. REF agreed to pay the insurance premium of R15 000, while other expenses, including the very high cost of transport (total R120 000), were undertaken by the Mazda Wildlife Fund.

The next question to be considered was the sex of the newcomers. Since the widespread search of the forest in 1980, during which only three elephants could be found, no further investigations had been undertaken. At that time the three consisted of an old bull, a mature cow, and a youngster aged approximately ten years, thought to be a bull. This young bull, now about 24 years of age, would be the key to the success of the experiment. It was therefore decided that the newcomers should both be female and should be selected from the cull which at that time took place annually in winter in the Kruger National Park. Although the Addo Elephant National Park, situated near Port Elizabeth, would seem a natural choice and the four-hour journey would have been much less stressful than the twenty-four-hour journey from the Kruger Park, there are certain drawbacks to Addo. The present large elephant herds there have all developed from a nucleus of only eleven animals – all that remained in fact after the slaughter, mentioned earlier, by Major Pretorius, which means that the gene pool of the Addo elephants is weaker than that of the Kruger Park elephants. A further drawback is that nearly all the females in Addo are tuskless. This would be a disadvantage in the forest, where such activities as digging for roots are common.

PREPARATIONS FOR THE NEW ARRIVALS

Elephants have an amazing ability to adapt to a wide variety of habitats – savanna, deserts, swamps, forests. Nevertheless, the changes facing these young Kruger Park elephants were formidable. They had lost the other members of their families in the cull, they were faced with a long journey, confined within a truck, and they had to deal with a major change of habitat, from the mostly warm savanna of the Kruger Park to the Knysna forest in a cold Cape winter. The difference in food, particularly the lack of grass, would add to the difficulties of successful adaptation.

It was essential therefore that everything be done to make the transition as easy as possible. To this end, a zoologist, Marion Garaï, was engaged as adviser. Marion had specialised in the study of the translocation of juvenile elephants and had acquired an extensive knowledge of this difficult operation. Furthermore, she had followed up many of these transfers and observed the effect on the elephants of the various arrangements and structures prepared for them. She had noticed that where the youngsters were closely confined and unable to put a reasonable distance between themselves and the people in the area, they became uneasy and showed signs of stress and aggression. However, where a spacious paddock was provided, in addition to a smaller pen or even without the pen, the elephants were far more ready to relax and accept the new environment. She therefore suggested that two bomas be constructed, one approximately 0,7 ha in size (roughly the size of a football pitch) and the other 3 ha, which would enclose a large section of indigenous forest. A fence would separate the two. The elephants would start off in the smaller boma where they could be monitored and where additional food could be provided. The smaller boma was situated so that two sides boasted a section of forest into which the elephants could disappear and experience a sense of privacy. Both bomas were surrounded by an electric fence.

Marion Garaï further recommended that, as elephants are highly social animals, three rather than two young elephants should be introduced. This would go some way to providing the family support group to which they had been accustomed in the Kruger Park. Professor Kader Asmal, the Minister of Water Affairs and Forestry, was approached and unhesitatingly gave his consent.

Marion Garaï

THE ELEPHANTS ARRIVE

15 July 1994. At 6 a.m. on a cold winter morning, a group of officials, media personnel, Rhino and Elephant Foundation and Wildlife Society representatives gath-

107

ered to await the arrival of the young elephants, who had started their long journey from the Kruger Park at 6 a.m. on the previous day. After a short delay the specially constructed Mazda Wildlife transporter came into view and drew up at the ramp leading into the boma. Doors were opened and a trunk appeared, feeling cautiously around the edges of the opening. About 20 minutes later the youngest of the elephants led the others down into the boma. All three immediately set off in line to the far side away from the assembled people, and disappeared into the narrow strip of forest. This was confirmation of Marion Garai's design of boma. The trees and bushes gave the youngsters a sense of security. Almost immediately they started to browse.

The oldest elephant, aged ten, had lost a tusk during the journey. Straightaway the forest workers christened her 'Aftand' after one of Knysna's most famous elephants who had lost part of his tusk while attacking a bulldozer. (Aftand is an Afrikaans word meaning tooth (tusk) off.) Later on her other tusk was found

The doors of the transporter are opened and a trunk carefully examines the opening. (Photo: M. Mackay)

The transporter draws
up beside the boma and
the tip of a trunk appears
over the side pointing
to the Mazda notice.
(Photo: M. Mackay)

Fern, the youngest,
leads the way into
the boma.
(Photo: Rhino & Elephant
Foundation)

Opposite (top): They line up for photographs. (Photo: Rhino & Elephant Foundation)

Opposite (below): The elephants set off in line astern to explore the trees and bushes lining their boma. (Photo: Rhino & Elephant Foundation)

Left: Aftande, the oldest, arrives last. (Photo: Rhino & Elephant Foundation)

Below: Two of the elephants exploring the outskirts of their piece of forest. After a cold dawn, the sun is just touching the tops of the trees. (Photo: M. Mackay)

lying in the boma. Thus her name changed to the plural 'Aftande' (teeth off)! These young elephants are now children of the forest and fynbos. What more appropriate names could there be than 'Erica', after the lovely flowering fynbos plants, the Ericas, for the second oldest elephant, aged nine, and for the youngest, aged eight, 'Fern' after the beautiful forest ferns?

The first phase was over, conducted with the expertise and care we have come to expect from National Parks Board operations.

Fern,
the youngest
of the new arrivals
from the Kruger Park.

SETTLING IN: THE START OF A NEW LIFE

The period after the arrival of the young elephants brought some of the worst weather ever remembered. Day after day pouring rain and bitter cold caused misery to the newcomers. When Chief Forester Martin Lucas or Assistant Forester Len du Plessis visited their charges in the morning, they found the elephants visibly shivering; Aftande even had frost on her back. Whenever the sun appeared, all three would stand in the clearing in the middle of the boma with their backs to the sun and lift each leg in turn while turning the sole up to the sun for warmth! After so much thought and care had been taken in the construction of the boma, it is surprising that no shelter of any kind was provided. Some kind of roof with a windbreak on one or two sides could have made all the difference.

During the initial period of discovering their new environment, Fern, although the youngest, seemed to be the most enterprising. The boma boasted a pool, a familiar and popular item in elephant life. The three approached the pool, but found themselves slipping and sliding on the edge. Aftande and Erica drew back, but Fern was not to be deterred. She stamped her feet in the mud until she had created a small pool for drinking and playing.

Chief Forester, Martin Lucas (right), and Assistant Forester Len du Plessis, Deepwalls Forest Station. They would be responsible for looking after the young elephants.

Supplementary feed consisting of horse cubes, a daily ration of ten bales of lucerne and a truckload of branches was supplied. The cubes and lucerne were placed in containers inside the fence near the ramp, but it was observed that the elephants were hesitant about approaching the area. Sensing that the reason might be connected with the ramp and memories of leaving home, of the loss of the family group, of the long journey and, finally, of walking down that ramp into a strange environment, the foresters considered possible solutions. With an understanding and sympathy which has always characterised their dealings with the young-sters, they spread a camouflage net over the offending ramp. It worked. Memories of an unpleasant experience faded away and the elephants tucked in to the extra food with enthusiasm.

During their stay in the smaller boma there was no lack of activity. In addition to feeding and browsing on their limited forest area, the elephants investigated other possible sources of entertainment. One day they were observed digging round the base of a yellowwood tree growing conveniently near the fence. Their purpose was unmistakable. They intended to push the tree over so that it would crash down on the fence, thus opening the way to freedom! However, this enterprising manoeuvre was short-lived. The foresters came in with a chain-saw and cut down the tree.

IMMOBILISATION – AGAIN

The elephants had been fitted with radio-transmitter collars before leaving the Kruger Park. Unfortunately, the transmitters proved to have insufficient power for forest conditions. It was therefore decided to replace them with more powerful transmitters – and a second immobilisation would have to take place. Thus, on 31 August 1994, Dr Cobus Raath, Head of Veterinary Services for the Kruger National Park, came down to Knysna and darted the elephants.

A bakkie (small truck) was used for the operation. This was less disturbing for the animals than seeing a person walk into the boma. The report by the Department of Forestry stated that all three animals went down in good positions with the minimum of trauma. Three veterinary scientists removed the collars during the hour in which the elephants remained

Dr Cobus Raath, Head of Veterinary Services for the Kruger National Park, fires the immobilising dart. (Photo: Department of Forestry)

The elephant is down. Johan Huisamen, one of the team of foresters, removes the dart. (Photo: Department of Forestry)

Small feet appear as the youngest elephant is rolled over during the fitting of the new radio collar. (Photo: Department of Forestry)

comatose and affixed new transmitters to them. After the administration of the antidote, the animals were on their feet within two minutes and had regrouped in three minutes. Dr Raath commented on the excellent condition of the young elephants and was satisfied that they were adapting to their new environment.

How much stress is caused during immobilisation by darting is debatable, but in the case of highly sensitive animals such as elephants it would appear to be considerable. The day after the operation, when Martin Lucas appeared with the same bakkie in the lane outside the boma, the elephants charged the fence in an attempt to get at the bakkie: they knew something unpleasant had happened. Perhaps they were still suffering from the after-effects. It is sad to relate that the new transmitters lasted for only six weeks before ceasing to function.

A STEP TOWARDS FREEDOM

On Friday morning, 2 September 1994, the fence between the two bomas was removed. Contrary to

The elephants were on their feet within two minutes — still a little unsteady. (Photo: Department of Forestry)

expectations, the elephants did not immediately take advantage of the opportunity for further exploration. It was two whole days before they summoned up the courage to cross the imaginary line into strange territory. Once this hurdle was overcome, however, they took off at an exhilarating gallop as if throwing caution to the winds, stopping only on reaching the fence at the eastern end.

During the days following the move, the young elephants appeared to be enjoying the much greater freedom of their new territory, using the natural waterholes, and feeding well. The supplementary feed was gradually reduced. It was observed that the elephants avoided the clearing in the original boma and used it only at night for drinking and feeding. It is highly probable that they associated the area with the immobilisation and felt that if they went there in the daytime, the unpleasant experience might occur all over again!

THE SEARCH

As late as October 1994, three months after the arrival of the Kruger Park elephants, an inquiry directed to the Department of Forestry as to the number of 'Knysna' elephants still remaining in the forest, elicited the same response: the three discovered in 1980 plus a calf born in January 1989. Doubts arose, however, within the Department of Forestry about the true state of affairs, and an intensive search was launched. Sixteen forest guards walking 200 metres apart combed the area known to comprise the elephants' favoured range. The result stunned the Knysna community. Only one indigenous elephant could be found and it was not the young bull: the sole survivor was a mature cow, aged about 45, the Matriarch, mother of the young calf. Once again, we had this inexplicable disappearance of elephants. This time the young calf, aged about six years, and the young bull, aged about twenty-five, had disappeared. In 1987 the young bull and a mature cow had been seen together by many people, yet this young animal, in the prime of life, who had grown up in the forest, had vanished, apparently without trace. Even allowing for mortality among calves, an accident to such an animal as the young bull would be most unlikely.

FREEDOM – AT LAST!

On 20 September, the gates of the larger boma were opened. Again, slowly and cautiously, the young elephants moved out into the big wide world of forest, fynbos, rivers and streams.

It was hoped that the elephants would turn in a westerly direction towards Gouna, but instead they moved east down the Ysterhoutrugpad, through a fynbos island, Dirk-se-eiland, to a small patch of forest, called Watervalbos, just above the Bitou River gorge. There they stayed for three to four weeks, spending two or three days reconnoitring one of the kloofs and then moving on to explore another. During this period a team of foresters and forest guards was carrying out non-stop monitoring of the elephants' movements. There was some concern as to whether they could negotiate the steep slopes of the gorge to reach the water, and so Dave Reynell, Forestry Information Officer, and Martin Lucas with two forest guards, climbed down into the gorge to find out. The result of this investigation showed that even young elephants can cope with steep and difficult ground: dung found along the riverbank proved that they had no difficulty in finding water. After their wanderings in the gorge, the young elephants retraced their route through Watervalbos and Dirk-se-eiland and settled down near the forest fringe at the western end of the island.

A rash of warning notices appeared in the forest and along the main road. Lorna Watt, Chairman of the Knysna Centre of the Wildlife Society, stands beside one of them.

118

While in the forest, the elephants developed the unfortunate habit of bark-stripping and were particularly hard on candlewood (*Pterocelastrus tricuspidatus*), sometimes leaving a trail of stripped, pole-sized trees with foliage untouched. This had never been a habit of the 'Knysna' elephants.

During this period of exploration in the vicinity of the Bitou River, the boundary of State land, there was some fear that the youngsters might embark on a trail which would lead them away from the forest and on to private land.

Approximately ten kilometres from Deepwalls as the crow flies – or as the elephant walks – lies the farm Eden Garden, owned by Ian and Lisette Withers, the home of two six-year-old elephants, Harry and Sally. These youngsters had been rescued from a game farm where animals were bred for hunting, and had been so neglected that Willie, the third member of the group, had succumbed to malnutrition. Although young elephants normally rely on their family group for their upbringing and well-being, these two have adopted Ian, Lisette and their family as a support group, and visible and happy communication exists between them. Harry and Sally are helping to create an ideal atmosphere for the environmental education programme that is being developed there. Ten kilometres is no distance for elephants to walk and it would be an interesting situation, to say the least, if the newcomers from the Kruger Park arrived at Eden Garden and tried to link up with Harry and Sally.

The results of bark-stripping by the young elephants. (Photo: M. Mackay)

Harry and Sally in 'conversation' with Ian and Lisette. (Photo: M. Mackay)

For the moment, however, the problem has not arisen. The elephants decided to return to the Deepwalls area.

A DESPERATE ENCOUNTER

On 8 October 1994 the three young elephants from the Kruger Park encountered the lone 'Knysna' elephant, the Matriarch, on the Uniondale road just south of the Ysterhoutrug picnic site. No one saw the encounter. Perhaps it happened during the night, perhaps at dawn – we shall never know. But the story was clearly written on the sandy surface of the road. It told of a scene of confusion and devastation as the elephants milled around in fear and bewilderment. Notice boards were torn down and a nearby gate bent and trampled. The Matriarch, who had suffered the disappearance of the other members of her group and who was used to the solitude of the forest, fled from the scene pursued by the young elephants, who were no doubt yearning for the family they had once known in the Kruger Park. That first day they covered about 30 km and the same distance again on the next day. Their route crisscrossed the Matriarch's normal territory backwards and forwards, as if she were trying to shake off the three young elephants following her. At the end of the fourth day, Fern, the youngest of the three, lay dead of stress-related pneumonia.

During the period of their stay in the smaller boma, Fern had frequently led the others in their activities, but this seemed to change after the second immobilisation. Perhaps, being the youngest, the operation had imposed more strain on her than was the case with the others. Aftande and Erica both came from the same family; Fern was not part of their group. The older elephants started to pick on her and perhaps they prevented her from obtaining enough food. She was relegated to the bottom of the pecking order; bullying is quite common among young elephants. The four days of violent activity and stress involved in the great distances that were covered after the encounter between the young elephants and the Matriarch finally proved too much.

The foresters and the community of Knysna were greatly saddened by the death of the youngest elephant.

120

Aftande and Erica stayed with the Matriarch for three months and during that time, according to Martin Lucas, she showed the youngsters her favourite elephant paths in the forest. However, just as it seemed that they would become a permanent group, a decision was made to part company. The young elephants returned to the fynbos island they had discovered during their first taste of freedom, and the Matriarch to her old haunts. It is not known who suggested the parting; possibly it was mutual. It is also possible that the Matriarch said to herself, "I just can't do with these youngsters any more. I must have some peace and quiet!" They have since joined up again from time to time, but for periods of only two or three days.

It is quite natural that elephants, accustomed to the open country of the savanna biome, should prefer full sun of the outskirts of the forest and the fynbos area. Yet this might not be the only reason. The arrival of the young elephants in bitterly cold and wet weather could have instilled in them a hearty dislike of the forest, with its dripping trees and gloomy weather. Had their first introduction to the forest been in pleasant, warm weather, the reaction might have been quite different.

Johan Huisamen (left), and Ian Withers survey the fynbos islands, a favourite haunt of the young elephants. (Photo: M. Mackay)

The forest is usually described as dense and, of course, much of it is, but there are many open spaces – the forest paths, roads such as the Kom-se-Pad between Deepwalls and Gouna, a great favourite with the 'Knysna' elephants, picnic sites, and areas surrounding the various forest stations. In addition, there have always been open fynbos areas within the forest. Many of these were planted with pine trees, but good news, recently received, is that some are being clear-felled and will not be replanted. Where this has already happened, the fynbos is recovering well. Critics who rate the forest as an unsuitable habitat for elephants emphasise the lack of grass as a major drawback. There are, however, areas where grass has been planted for the forest horses, and also quite extensive stretches of grass in the region of picnic sites, yet the elephants have generally ignored them.

THE PROBLEM OF WANDERING ELEPHANTS

The outskirts of the forest and the fynbos islands became the favoured range of the young elephants. Although there is no shortage of State land in that area, problems arose through the lack of a boundary fence. There was nothing to stop the elephants from wandering off State land on to private property, and this is just what they did. They crossed the forest boundary, the Bitou River, and found a cultivated field. This field became a 5-star restaurant in the opinion of Aftande and Erica, and they returned to it again and again. Fortunately, the farmer concerned had no objection to their visitations. In fact, the farmers in that whole area were very tolerant of the young elephants. Nevertheless, this was an extremely worrying development. Problems of insurance could arise once they were off State property should any damage be caused. Word spread quickly that the elephants had been seen and some uncaring people harassed and frightened the youngsters, causing them to wander far from their

Fynbos,
forest and mountains
in the Millwood area.
(Photo: D. Mackay)

122

known territory. Martin Lucas and his team kept in constant touch, ready to deal with any emergency. Then, to everybody's relief, the wanderers turned back into the forest and headed for their old haunts in the Deepwalls area. One very interesting fact was observed. During their quite extensive wanderings, the young elephants never once damaged a fence. When they wished to change direction, they waited until they found an open gate. Obviously they still remembered the electric fence which had surrounded the boma.

This commendably disciplined behaviour lasted for two years, until June 1996, when damage to a fence was reported. They had discovered that not all fences are electrified!

AN OVERVIEW

During October 1995, the Department of Water Affairs and Forestry issued an Overview of the elephant relocation project. This document gave a summary of the events following the arrival of the young elephants and stated that, until December 1994, staff of the Department were very satisfied with the reintroduction programme. However, it was at this point that the 'combing' operation took place which produced the dismal news that only one indigenous elephant, a mature female, had survived.

The Overview presented various options for consideration at a meeting held on 5 October 1995, attended by Cape Nature Conservation, Rhino and Elephant Foundation, The Wildlife Society, Du Toit Game Services, and other interested parties:

Option One:
Bring in some more elephants with a view to establishing a *viable* population, i.e. family groups with sexually mature bulls – population maintenance.

The Elephant Working Group decided to go for this option with (perhaps) continual top-ups of the population, in the hope that it might work.

Erica

123

The viability of this option has now been weakened as a result of:

a) Further confirmations of the habitat problem: only one Knysna elephant remains.
b) The loss of the 'Knysna' elephant gene pool (transmission of genes from a female being less effective and slower).
c) The fact that there is only one remaining Knysna elephant makes the project less viable.
d) The long-term prospects of success have diminished.

Forestry would oppose a motion of this nature.

Option Two:

Introduce some more young elephants, in the knowledge that the project would *never* be ecologically viable. An artificial option.

Forestry would be prepared to continue with this option if *fully* funded by those advocating it (i.e., the people of Knysna).

In this event, the project could proceed:

a) Now, in the hope of preserving the Knysna gene pool or
b) After a further period of monitoring the movement/ behaviour patterns of the two young elephants presently in the forest.

Option Three:

To maintain the *status quo.*

Option Four:

a) To remove the relocated elephants immediately or
b) To remove the relocated elephants when problems arise.

Forestry decided to support Options 3 and 4b.

After discussion, it was agreed that the behaviour of the two remaining elephants should be monitored for another year. The project could then be reviewed at the end of that period.

1996 – THE KRUGER PARK ELEPHANTS – QUO VADIS?

Two years have passed since the arrival of the young elephants in July 1994. At that time the foresters were confident that at least three elephants, a mature cow, her calf, a young bull and possibly an old bull, were still active and alive in the forest. The reality, discovered a

few months later, was that only one elephant, an elderly female – the Matriarch – had survived and that all the elephants remaining in the forest were female.

To bring in a sexually mature bull of an age which the Matriarch would accept for mating could be dangerous for people walking in the forest. Furthermore, serious hazards could arise if he walked out of the forest on to private land. I wonder if I am a lone voice crying in the wilderness in suggesting that Option Two of the Overview perhaps merits further consideration? If four more young elephants were translocated, two bulls and one cow about the age of the existing youngsters, plus a female a few years older to act as the leader and matriarch, the additional numbers, together with the existing Kruger Park elephants, could constitute a stable family group, which could then give the support, social interaction and stimulation so necessary for the development and well-being of young elephants.

Although in normal elephant society the Matriarch would probably not accept a young bull as a mate, the circumstances existing in the Knysna forest are far from

The Matriarch emerges from a forest path. (Photo: Johan Huisamen, Department of Forestry)

normal. Therefore, the possibility cannot be ruled out of the Matriarch mating with one of the young bulls after they have become sexually mature.

Meanwhile, Aftande and Erica are roaming the forest on their own like a couple of wayward teenagers. This unnatural situation could lead to abnormal behaviour. It is not fair to the young elephants, and a decision should be made without delay, either to bring in more elephants, or relocate Aftande and Erica to a private game reserve where other elephants are already established.

THE STRANGE CASE OF THE DISAPPEARING ELEPHANTS

This sounds like the title of a Sherlock Homes story, and perhaps an investigator with the skills of that famous detective is just what we need in the Knysna forests.

Here are the facts:

- In 1970 Nick Carter's survey recorded the presence

of eleven elephants, and this estimate was confirmed by two surveys which took place just prior to Nick's year-long investigation.

- In 1980 an intensive search produced only three elephants – an old bull, a cow, and a young bull.
- In only ten years, eight elephants had disappeared. Three of these were old bulls who had lived to full term. Their deaths could be natural, but the remaining five were young to middle-aged animals.
- In 1989 a calf was born.
- In December 1994 a search in the form of a 'combing' operation took place. Only one elephant, a cow about 45 years old, was found. Had they lived, the calf would be five years old and the young bull, thought to have been born in 1970, would be 24 years old – in the prime of life.

A very strange feature of this mystery is that, although remains of old elephants have been found, only one skeleton of a young animal has been discovered with the exception of very young calves which have met an untimely end. What happened? Where are these young elephants?

We have been concentrating on the problems of the young Kruger Park elephants, but what about the needs of the Matriarch? According to Martin Lucas, she is showing signs of deeply disturbed behaviour. She is spending most of her time roaming in the vicinity of the Deepwalls Forest Station, particularly the area where she first encountered the young elephants. She has on several occasions wrecked the same gate which suffered during that first meeting and regularly rearranges the noticeboards nearby. Is she looking for the young elephants? Is this strange behaviour a protest against loneliness?

The Matriarch wreck the gate and regularly re-arranges the notice boards.

THE MATRIARCH – THE LAST KNYSNA ELEPHANT – THE LAST OF A GREAT DYNASTY

The thousands of elephants which once roamed the forests and the southern Cape coast have been wantonly destroyed by man's cruelty and greed. But for a few notable and noble exceptions, no one was interested in these highly intelligent animals except to kill them. There was no move to conserve them, or to appreciate their remarkable qualities. In the enchanting book

Among the Elephants by Iain and Oria Douglas-Hamilton, Oria writes:

"By photographing elephants day in and day out, I soon discovered that they showed many of the old-fashioned virtues, loyalty, protection and affection towards each other . . . For elephants, the unity of a family is one of the most important things in their lives. I was deeply moved by the constant affection and care which they showed every day within the families; mothers, daughters, sisters, babies, all touching and communicating with each other in a very loving way."

It has been said that since there is apparently only one 'Knysna' elephant remaining in the forest, any further action, such as the introduction of more elephants, could not be justified as a conservation measure and would be a case of merely maintaining a tourist attraction.

Of course, elephants are a source of wonder and excitement to visitors, but there is much more than this involved in their presence. When people walk in the forest, their senses are alert because they know that elephants are present even if they never see them. They become much more aware of the other wonders of the forest – of the drone of the cicadas, the persistent calling of the frogs, the beauty of the lichens and the colourful fungi, the secretive birds, the exquisite orchids and other delicate flowers of the forest, the glory of the fynbos, and the majesty of the great trees. No longer is the walk just a trudge along a forest path: it becomes a fascinating experience for those willing to pause and look and listen.

The creation of a small, viable herd of elephants is now admittedly more difficult, but it is not impossible. Some will be reluctant to take a chance on further action, but the introduction of the three young elephants from the Kruger National Park in July 1994 was an experiment fraught with possible disasters. These have not happened, and had there, in fact, been a group of indigenous elephants, including two youngsters, available to link up with the newcomers, as was thought at the time, we might now be seeing a rejuvenated group, a nucleus of young elephants with the chance of a successful future.

The title of this chapter is also the title of the picture of the last Knysna elephant painted by Sheila Cooper Collins: 'The Matriarch – the last Knysna elephant – the

last of a great dynasty'. If no other plan is made, she will continue her lonely wanderings until she, too, disappears. If that time comes, the imprint of those massive feet on the soft earth of the forest, the piles of dung, the sound of a breaking branch, the stillness of the forest as the walker, with fearful excitement, strains to hear the sounds which mean that elephants are near – such moments of magic will have gone for ever.

Many people do not believe that only one 'Knysna' elephant remains. They are convinced that in the vastness of the forest there are still elephants leading their lives, away from the sound of humans.

In 1987 a mature cow with her companion the young bull was seen by many people. In 1989 this cow was found dead. According to a report in the *Knysna/Plett Herald* dated 7 September 1989, the then Regional Director of the Department of Environmental Affairs and Forestry, Mr Danie Muller, made the following comments: "The skeletal remains could not be those of the mother of the calf now known to be in the forest. Firstly, the calf is too young to be without its mother, and it is known that the calf is still alive. Secondly, the remains are thought to be those of a very aged cow which died about a year ago, and thirdly, the tusks on

Tusks of the elephant found dead in 1989. They are mounted in the office of the Deepwalls Forest Station.
(Photo: M. Mackay)

the skeleton, are much smaller than those of the mother of the calf." (The tusks are mounted in the office at the Deepwalls Forestry Station. They match those of the elephant seen by hikers and photographed by Jons Flentgie.)

In October 1990 one of the forest guards saw the cow and the calf. In other words, the existing elephant, the Matriarch, is the mother of the calf, born in 1989, and *two* mature cows had been roaming the forest, not one, as everybody thought.

If such a mistake could occur, is it not possible that an elephant, perhaps the young bull, has withdrawn to lead a solitary life in the deep kloofs, the wild areas, parts of which are impenetrable, and perhaps, one day, might return and seek the companionship of the Matriarch?

Not even the foresters, who spend their lives in the forest, have the answers to these mysteries of the elephants and their forest home.

Appendix A
ENJOYING THE FOREST

The forest stations along the Garden Route have done a magnificent job. They have provided beautiful picnic sites among fine old trees or alongside streams, created hiking trails and walks, and numbered the trees so that all may learn to recognise and enjoy them.

The Outeniqua and Tsitsikamma trails, with their varied and lovely scenery and well-appointed overnight huts, give hikers an unforgettable experience of forest, fynbos and mountains. These trails can be split up into hikes of two or three days if time or energy is limited. For those who prefer not to carry a heavy pack, there are walks ranging from an hour or so to all day.

As you walk through the forest, pause and listen. Almost certainly you will hear frogs, perhaps the chatter of a party of Redbilled Woodhoopoe making its way through the forest, or see the glorious crimson flash of the Knysna Lourie flying from tree to tree. If you are really lucky, you might see one of our most beautiful birds, the Narina Trogon, sitting quietly on a branch. The Narina Trogon was named by Le Vaillant after a Hottentot girl whose beauty he greatly admired.

Turn over a decaying log and see what creatures live beneath or in it. You are most likely to find a scorpion, so be careful how you handle the log, but you might also find *Peripatus*, 30–40 mm long, a strange little creature like a small, grey caterpillar with horns. A relic from the primeval past, it is a missing link between the worms and insects. When disturbed or threatened, it squirts a sticky liquid from glands in the head. This liquid is capable of immobilising most small creatures and is probably used by *Peripatus* to capture its prey. Now have a look at the log itself. It is very important. It helps to slow down run-off water. Matter such as leaves and seeds drift against it, forming a patch of compost where seedlings of grass, shrubs and trees can grow in its moist shade. As the log decomposes, it turns into humus; bacteria and fungi appear and the log becomes a little world of food for insects such as termites and wood-boring beetles. The dead log has become a vital, living thing – the first link in the food chain for both plants and animals. Be sure to put the log back exactly as you found it or you could cause disaster to an entire colony of creatures.

Remember, also, wherever you are – beach, picnic site, mountains or forest – TAKE ONLY PICTURES, LEAVE ONLY FOOTPRINTS.

"Let no one say and say it to your shame
That there was beauty here until you came."

(Kipling)

Appendix B
FOREST TREES

The Dendrological Foundation, Pretoria assumed responsibility for a standard tree list. The following numbers refer to those published in their booklet entitled *National list of indigenous trees.*

2	*Alsophila capensis*	Bos boomvaring/Forest tree fern
16	*Podocarpus falcatus*	Kalander/Outeniqua yellowwood
18	*Podocarpus latifolius*	Geelhout/Yellowwood
32	*Strelitzia alba*	Kaapse wildepiesang/Cape wild banana
39	*Celtis africana*	Witstinkhout/White stinkwood
50	*Ficus capensis*	Wildevyeboom or Besemtrosvy/Wild fig or Broom cluster fig
74	*Faurea macnaughtonii*	Terblans
118	*Ocotea bullata*	Stinkhout/Stinkwood
139	*Pittosporum viridiflorum*	Witboekenhout/White beech
140	*Cunonia capensis*	Rooiels/Red alder
141	*Platylophus trifoliatus*	Witels/White alder
142	*Trichocladus crinitus*	Onderbos/Black witch-hazel
147	*Prunus africana*	Rooistinkhout/Red stinkwood
221	*Virgilia oroboides*	Keurboom
254	*Fagara davyi*	Perdepram/Knobwood
256	*Calodendrum capense*	Wildekastaiing/Cape chestnut
261	*Vepris undulata*	Witysterhout/White ironwood
298	*Ekebergia capensis*	Essenhout/Cape ash
307	*Lachnostylis hirta*	Koolhout/Coalwood
380	*Rhus chirindensis*	Bostaaibos/Red currant
388.1	*Rhus lucida*	Rooitaaibos/Glossy currant
397	*Ilex mitis*	Without/Cape holly
398	*Maytenus acuminata*	Rooisybas/Red silky bark
401	*Maytenus peduncularis*	Swarthout/Indigenous blackwood
409	*Pterocelastrus tricuspidatus*	Kershout/Candlewood
413	*Cassine eucleiformis*	Witsybas/White silky bark
414	*Cassine peragua*	Bastersaffraan/Bastard saffron
415	*Cassine papillosa*	Saffraan/Saffron
422	*Apodytes dimidiata*	Witpeer/White pear
451	*Scutia myrtina*	Katdoring/Cat-thorn

479	Ochna arborea	Rooihout/Cape plane
494	Kiggelaria africana	Vaderlandsrooihout/Wild peach
496	Scolopia mundii	Rooipeer/Red pear
498	Scolopia zeyheri	Wolwedoring/Thorn pear
503	Trimeria grandifolia	Wildemoerbei/Wild mulberry
513	Olinia ventosa	Hardepeer/Hard pear
570	Curtisia dentata	Assegaai/Assegai
578	Rapanea melanophloeos	Boekenhout/Cape beech
579	Sideroxylon inerme	Melkhout/Milkwood
603	Diospyros dichrophylla	Tolbos/Monkey plum
611	Diospyros whyteana	Bostolbos/Forest monkey plum
615	Chionanthus foveolatus	Fynblaarysterhout/Ornate-leaved ironwood
618	Olea capensis ssp. capensis	Basterysterhout/Bastard ironwood
618.2	Olea capensis ssp. macrocarpa	Ysterhout/Ironwood
624	Strychnos decussata	Kaapse Kiaat/Cape teak
634	Nuxia floribunda	Vlier/Wild elder
636	Buddleja saligna	Witolienhout/Bastard olive
637	Buddleja salviifolia	Saliehout/Wild sage
641	Gonioma kamassi	Kammassie/Kamassi
670	Halleria lucida	Notsung/Tree fuchsia
688	Burchellia bubalina	Wildegranaat/Wild pomegranate
693	Rothmannia capensis	Wildekatjiepiering/Wild gardenia
708	Canthium inerme	Bokdrol/Turkey-berry
710	Canthium mundianum	Klipels/Rock alder
711	Canthium obovatum	Kwar/Quar
733	Tarchonanthus camphoratus	Wildesalie/Camphor-bush

Appendix C
FOREST BIRDS

Birdwatching in the forest is difficult owing to the dense canopy above, but a sudden call or movement often betrays the birds' presence. Then patience is needed, so sit down and watch, particularly where there is a break in the canopy or a thinner patch of trees.

Below is a list of birds, excluding water birds, which may be seen in the forest. All numbers relate to *Roberts' Birds of Southern Africa* (1993).

63	Ardea melanocephala	Blackheaded Heron
81	Scopus umbretta	Hamerkop
94	Bostrychia hagedash	Hadeda Ibis
128	Aviceda cuculoides	Cuckoo Hawk
141	Stephanoaetus coronatus	Crowned Eagle
150	Buteo trizonatus	Forest Buzzard
152	Buteo rufofuscus	Jackal Buzzard
155	Accipiter rufiventris	Redbreasted Sparrowhawk
158	Accipiter melanoleucus	Black Sparrowhawk

160	*Accipiter tachiro*	African Goshawk
169	*Polyboroides typus*	Gymnogene
198	*Francolinus afer*	Rednecked Francolin
218	*Sarothrura elegans*	Buffspotted Flufftail
350	*Columba arquatrix*	Rameron Pigeon
352	*Streptopelia semitorquata*	Redeyed Dove
354	*Streptopelia capicola*	Cape Turtle Dove
355	*Streptopelia senegalensis*	Laughing Dove
358	*Turtur chalcospilos*	Greenspotted Dove
359	*Turtur tympanistria*	Tambourine Dove
360	*Aplopelia larvata*	Cinnamon Dove
370	*Tauraco corythaix*	Knysna Lourie
377	*Cuculus solitarius*	Redchested Cuckoo
382	*Clamator jacobinus*	Jacobin Cuckoo
384	*Chrysococcyx cupreus*	Emerald Cuckoo
394	*Strix woodfordii*	Wood Owl
400	*Bubo capensis*	Cape Eagle Owl
401	*Bubo africanus*	Spotted Eagle Owl
405	*Caprimulgus pectoralis*	Fierynecked Nightjar
427	*Apaloderma narina*	Narina Trogon
452	*Phoeniculus purpureus*	Redbilled Woodhoopoe
475	*Indicator variegatus*	Scalythroated Honeyguide
476	*Indicator minor*	Lesser Honeyguide
484	*Campethera notata*	Knysna Woodpecker
488	*Mesopicos griseocephalus*	Olive Woodpecker
536	*Psalidoprocne holomelas*	Black Saw-wing Swallow
540	*Coracina caesia*	Grey Cuckooshrike
541	*Dicrurus adsimilis*	Forktailed Drongo
545	*Oriolus larvatus*	Blackheaded Oriole
550	*Corvus albicollis*	Whitenecked Raven
566	*Pycnonotus capensis*	Cape Bulbul
569	*Phyllastrephus terrestris*	Terrestrial Bulbul
572	*Andropadus importunus*	Sombre Bulbul
577	*Turdus olivaceus*	Olive Thrush
598	*Cossypha dichroa*	Chorister Robin
601	*Cossypha caffra*	Cape Robin
606	*Pogonocichla stellata*	Starred Robin
640	*Bradypterus sylvaticus*	Knysna Warbler
644	*Seicercus ruficapillus*	Yellowthroated Warbler
645	*Apalis thoracica*	Barthroated Apalis
657	*Camaroptera brachyura*	Bleating Warbler
690	*Muscicapa adusta*	Dusky Flycatcher
700	*Batis capensis*	Cape Batis
708	*Trochocercus cyanomelas*	Bluemantled Flycatcher
710	*Terpsiphone viridis*	Paradise Flycatcher
736	*Laniarius ferrugineus*	Southern Boubou

740	*Dryscopus cubla*	Puffback
768	*Lamprotornis corruscus*	Blackbellied Starling
783	*Nectarinia chalybea*	Lesser Doublecollared Sunbird
785	*Nectarinia afra*	Greater Doublecollared Sunbird
792	*Nectarinia amethystina*	Black Sunbird
793	*Anthreptes collaris*	Collared Sunbird
796	*Zosterops pallidus*	Cape White-eye
873	*Serinus scotops*	Forest Canary
874	*Pseudochloroptila totta*	Cape Siskin

Appendix D
MAMMALS

Amblysomus hottentotus	Hottentot golden mole
Amblysomus iris	Knysna golden mole
Aonyx capensis	Cape clawless otter
Atilax puludinosus	Water mongoose
Cercopithecus pygerythrus	Vervet monkey
Chlorotalpa duthieae	Duthie's golden mole
Crocidura flavescens	Giant musk shrew
Cryptomys hottentotus	Common molerat
Eptesicus capensis	Cape serotine bat
Felis caracal	Caracal
Felis lybica	African wild cat
Genetta tigrina	Large-spotted genet
Georychus capensis	Cape molerat
Graphiurus murinus	Woodland dormouse
Herpestes ichneumon	Cape ichneumon
Herpestes pulverulentus	Cape grey mongoose
Hystrix africae-australis	Porcupine
Ictonyx striatus	Striped polecat
Kerivoula lanosa	Woolly bat
Mellivora capensis	Honey badger
Myosorex longicaudatus	Longtailed forest shrew
Myosorex varius	Forest shrew
Panthera pardus	Leopard
Papio ursinus	Baboon
Philantomba moticola	Blue duiker
Pipistrellus kuhlii	Kuhl's bat
Potamochoerus porcus	Bush pig
Praomys verreauxii	Cape mouse
Rousettus aegyptiacus	Cape fruit bat
Suncus infinitesimus	Least dwarf shrew
Taphozous mauritianus	Tomb bat
Thamnomys dolichurus	Forest mouse
Tragelaphus scriptus	Cape bushbuck

Appendix E
REPTILES

Amplorhinus multimaculatus	Many-spotted snake
Bitis arietans arietans	Puff adder
Boaedon fuliginosus fuliginosus	Brown house snake
Causus rhombeatus	Night adder
Crotaphopeltis hotamboeia hotamboeia	Herald snake
Dasypeltis scabra	Common egg-eater
Dispholidus typus	Boomslang
Duberria lutrix lutrix	Slug-eater
Lamprophis aurora	Aurora house snake
Lamprophis inornatus	Olive house snake
Lycodonomorphus rufulus	Brown water snake
Philothamnus hoplogaster	Green water snake
Pseudaspis cana	Mole snake
Bradypodiun damaranum	Knysna dwarf chameleon
Mabuya capensis	Cape skink
Pachydactylus bibronii	Bibron's gecko
Pedioplanis lineoocellata	Spotted sand lizard

Appendix F
AMPHIBIANS

Afrixalus knysnae	Knysna leaf-folding frog
Breviceps fuscus	Plain rain frog
Bufo rangeri	Raucous toad
Cacosternum boettgeri	Common caco
Cacosternum nanum	Bronze caco
Heleophryne regis	Southern ghost frog
Hyperolius horstocki	Arum lily frog
Rana angolensis	Common river frog
Rana fuscigula	Cape river frog
Semnodactylas wealii	Rattling frog
Strongylopus fasciatus	Striped stream frog
Strongylopus grayii	Clicking stream frog
Xenopus laevis	Common platanna